The Mysteries of Historical Deaths: Investigating the Unsolved Enigmas

Shah Rukh

Published by Shah Rukh, 2024.

While every precaution has been taken in the preparation of this book, the publisher assumes no responsibility for errors or omissions, or for damages resulting from the use of the information contained herein.

THE MYSTERIES OF HISTORICAL DEATHS: INVESTIGATING THE UNSOLVED ENIGMAS

First edition. July 6, 2024.

Copyright © 2024 Shah Rukh.

Written by Shah Rukh.

Table of Contents

Prologue

Throughout the annals of history, humanity has been captivated by the allure of the unknown and the inexplicable. The shadows of uncertainty loom large over certain events, casting a shroud of mystery that refuses to dissipate with time. "The Mysteries of Historical Deaths: Investigating the Unsolved Enigmas" delves into the heart of these shadows, exploring the lives and untimely ends of individuals whose deaths have left an indelible mark on the collective consciousness.

In every culture and era, stories of unexplained deaths and disappearances have sparked curiosity and fear. From ancient times to the modern age, the passing of figures like Alexander the Great and Princess Diana have sparked countless theories and debates, each attempting to piece together the fragments of truth hidden within the enigma. This book embarks on a journey through such cases, each a unique tale of intrigue, speculation, and the unending quest for answers.

As we turn the pages of history, we encounter figures whose lives were marked by brilliance and whose deaths were cloaked in ambiguity. The vanishing of Amelia Earhart, the disappearance of the Roanoke Colony, and the tragic demise of Marilyn Monroe each present a puzzle that has yet to be definitively solved. These stories, often tinged with conspiracy and filled with unanswered questions, offer a glimpse into the complexities of the human experience and the limits of our understanding.

This compilation is not merely an examination of death but a celebration of the enduring human spirit's quest for knowledge. It is an invitation to ponder the what-ifs and explore the myriad possibilities that surround these historical mysteries. Each chapter is a testament to the unresolved and a tribute to the enigmatic individuals whose stories continue to fascinate and perplex.

Join us as we step into the past, unraveling the threads of history's most perplexing deaths and disappearances. Through careful investigation and thoughtful consideration, "The Mysteries of Historical Deaths: Investigating the Unsolved Enigmas" seeks to shed light on the dark corners of history and bring us closer to understanding the unfathomable.

In the pursuit of these truths, we honor the memories of those who have left us with more questions than answers. May their stories inspire us to look beyond the surface, to question, and to seek the truth in all its forms. Welcome to a journey through history's greatest unsolved enigmas.

Chapter 1: The Vanishing of Amelia Earhart

The vanishing of Amelia Earhart is one of the most perplexing mysteries in the annals of aviation and has captivated imaginations for decades. Born on July 24, 1897, in Atchison, Kansas, Earhart was a pioneering aviator, a symbol of the burgeoning field of aviation, and a beacon of inspiration for women in a male-dominated era. Her disappearance during an attempt to circumnavigate the globe in 1937 remains a topic of intense speculation and research, embodying both the spirit of adventure and the enigma of unsolved historical puzzles.

Earhart's ambition was apparent early in her life. After attending a stunt-flying exhibition, she took her first flight in December 1920 with pilot Frank Hawks. This experience ignited her passion for aviation, leading her to take flying lessons and, eventually, to set records and break barriers. In 1928, she became the first woman to fly across the Atlantic as a passenger. Not satisfied with this, she piloted a solo transatlantic flight in 1932, becoming the first woman and only the second person to do so, after Charles Lindbergh. These accomplishments solidified her status as an aviation icon and propelled her into the public eye.

Earhart's attempt to fly around the world in 1937 was a grand and perilous endeavor. Alongside her navigator, Fred Noonan, she embarked on this journey in a Lockheed Electra 10E. Their plan was to cover approximately 29,000 miles, starting from Oakland, California, traveling eastward across South America, Africa, India, and Southeast Asia, before crossing the Pacific. By the time they reached Lae, New Guinea, they had successfully covered about 22,000 miles, leaving the challenging Pacific crossing as the final leg of their journey.

On July 2, 1937, Earhart and Noonan took off from Lae for Howland Island, a tiny, uninhabited island in the central Pacific Ocean, which was a critical refueling stop. This leg of the journey, spanning 2,556 miles, was fraught with difficulties, including navigation challenges and the limitations of radio communication at the time. Earhart's aircraft was equipped with a two-way radio, but the technology was rudimentary, and the vastness of the Pacific Ocean made consistent communication challenging. The Coast Guard cutter Itasca was stationed near Howland Island to provide radio navigation and assist in guiding the plane to its destination.

The flight started well, with regular radio transmissions being received by the Itasca. However, as the aircraft neared Howland Island, communication became erratic and problematic. Earhart's last known transmission, recorded at 8:43 a.m., indicated that she believed she was near Howland but could not see the island and was low on fuel. Despite frantic efforts by the Itasca to establish communication and guide the plane to safety, Earhart's signals faded into silence, and no further transmissions were received.

The immediate response to Earhart's disappearance was a massive search operation, one of the most extensive of its kind at the time. The U.S. Navy and Coast Guard, alongside civilian vessels and aircraft, scoured thousands of square miles of ocean in a desperate attempt to find any trace of the lost aviators. Despite these efforts, no conclusive evidence of the plane or its occupants was found, leading to a wide array of theories and speculations about their fate.

One prominent theory suggests that Earhart and Noonan ran out of fuel and crashed into the Pacific Ocean near Howland Island. This hypothesis is supported by the lack of confirmed sightings and the limitations of their aircraft's fuel capacity. The vastness of the ocean and the depth of the waters in the region would make it incredibly difficult to locate the wreckage, even with modern search technologies.

Another compelling theory posits that Earhart and Noonan, unable to locate Howland Island, flew on until they reached Gardner Island (now Nikumaroro), part of the Phoenix Islands. This theory gained traction with the discovery of artifacts on Nikumaroro, including a piece of metal believed to be part of Earhart's aircraft, and reports of skeletal remains that some believe could belong to the aviators. The International Group for Historic Aircraft Recovery (TIGHAR) has conducted multiple expeditions to Nikumaroro, uncovering various artifacts and evidence that suggest a possible human presence during the time of Earhart's disappearance. However, definitive proof linking these findings to Earhart remains elusive.

Some more sensational theories suggest that Earhart and Noonan were captured by the Japanese, possibly after crash-landing on the Marshall Islands or another location within Japanese territory. Proponents of this theory argue that Earhart may have been spying for the U.S. government, a claim bolstered by anecdotal evidence and unverified accounts from the period. However, there is little concrete evidence to support this scenario, and it remains largely in the realm of conjecture.

Over the years, various expeditions and research efforts have continued to search for definitive answers. Advances in technology, including sonar mapping and underwater exploration, have enabled more thorough searches of the ocean floor, yet no conclusive evidence has emerged. The mystery of Amelia Earhart's disappearance continues to fuel speculation, academic research, and public fascination.

The legacy of Amelia Earhart extends beyond her mysterious disappearance. She remains a symbol of courage, determination, and the relentless pursuit of dreams. Her achievements in aviation and her role as a trailblazer for women in the field have left an indelible mark on history. Despite the mystery surrounding her fate, Earhart's contributions to aviation and her spirit of adventure continue to inspire generations of pilots, explorers, and dreamers worldwide.

The vanishing of Amelia Earhart embodies the human fascination with the unknown and the allure of unresolved mysteries. It serves as a reminder of the perils of exploration and the limits of human knowledge, even in an age of advanced technology and global communication. As long as the question of what happened to Amelia Earhart remains unanswered, it will continue to be a topic of intrigue and speculation, a story that captures the imagination and stirs the soul.

Chapter 2: The Disappearance of the Roanoke Colony

The disappearance of the Roanoke Colony is one of the most enduring and intriguing mysteries in American history, involving the unexplained vanishing of a group of English settlers in the late 16th century. The story of Roanoke begins with England's ambition to establish a permanent settlement in the New World, reflecting both the aspirations and the challenges of early colonial endeavors. Situated on Roanoke Island, in what is now North Carolina, the colony's fate has spawned numerous theories and extensive research, yet it remains unresolved, shrouded in mystery and speculation.

The Roanoke Colony, also known as the Lost Colony, was founded in 1587 by a group of 115 settlers led by John White. This was not the first English attempt to establish a presence on Roanoke Island; an earlier expedition in 1585, sponsored by Sir Walter Raleigh and led by Ralph Lane, had ended in failure due to conflicts with Native American tribes and difficulties in sustaining the colony. Learning from these initial setbacks, the new settlers aimed to establish a more permanent community. John White, who was appointed as the governor of the colony, played a key role in the expedition, bringing along his daughter, Eleanor Dare, and her husband, Ananias Dare. The birth of Virginia Dare, the first English child born in the Americas, marked a hopeful beginning for the fledgling colony.

Upon their arrival, the settlers faced numerous challenges, including a lack of food, hostile relations with indigenous tribes, and the harsh and unfamiliar environment. Despite these difficulties, they attempted to build a new life on the island, constructing homes and striving to establish agriculture. However, the settlers soon realized that they needed additional supplies and reinforcements from England to sustain their efforts. In August 1587, John White departed for England to procure the necessary resources, leaving behind his family and fellow colonists with the promise of a swift return.

White's return to Roanoke, however, was delayed by several years due to a combination of factors, including the outbreak of the Anglo-Spanish War and the pressing need for ships and resources to defend England against the Spanish Armada. These circumstances made it difficult for White to secure a passage back to the New World. It wasn't until 1590, three years after his departure, that he was able to return to Roanoke Island. Upon his arrival, White found the settlement deserted, with no trace of the colonists he had left behind.

The only clues to the colonists' fate were the word "CROATOAN" carved into a post of the fort and the letters "CRO" inscribed on a nearby tree. These inscriptions suggested a possible relocation to Croatoan Island (now known as Hatteras Island), which was home to a Native American tribe of the same name. White interpreted the carvings as a sign that the settlers had moved to the island in search of safety and sustenance. However, adverse weather conditions and dwindling supplies prevented White from conducting a thorough search, and he was forced to return to England without any concrete answers.

The enigmatic disappearance of the Roanoke colonists has given rise to a plethora of theories and speculations over the centuries. One prevailing theory is that the settlers assimilated with local Native American tribes, such as the Croatoan or other nearby groups like the Chesapeake or the Lumbee. This theory is supported by oral histories and the accounts of later explorers who encountered Native American tribes with European features and customs, suggesting intermarriage and cultural integration.

Another theory posits that the colonists attempted to relocate to a more favorable area but perished due to harsh conditions, lack of supplies, or conflicts with Native American tribes. This idea is bolstered by the fact that Roanoke Island was not ideally suited for agriculture and the settlers likely struggled to sustain themselves without additional support from England. Some researchers have suggested that the colonists may have tried to move inland towards more fertile areas, such as the Chowan River, but encountered insurmountable obstacles.

There are also theories that propose more sinister outcomes. Some suggest that the settlers fell victim to a massacre by hostile Native American tribes or Spanish forces, who were active in the region and wary of English encroachment on their claimed territories. However, there is little concrete evidence to support these claims, and no definitive signs of violence or conflict have been uncovered at the site.

In recent years, archaeological research has provided new insights into the fate of the Roanoke colonists. Excavations on Roanoke Island and nearby areas have uncovered artifacts that may be linked to the missing settlers, including English pottery, tools, and weapons. One significant discovery is the unearthing of a map, known as the "Virginea Pars" map, which was created by John White and features a patch that conceals a symbol believed to indicate a fort or settlement in the Chesapeake Bay area. This finding has led some researchers to speculate that the colonists may have attempted to establish a new settlement further north, in line with the original plans for a more permanent colony.

Additionally, recent excavations on Hatteras Island have uncovered European artifacts dating from the late 16th century, including a signet ring, a sword hilt, and pieces of pottery. These findings lend credence to the theory that at least some of the Roanoke colonists may have relocated to the island and integrated with the Croatoan tribe. However, while these discoveries are intriguing, they do not provide conclusive evidence of the colonists' ultimate fate.

The story of the Roanoke Colony is more than just a tale of disappearance; it is a reflection of the broader context of early European colonization efforts in North America. The challenges faced by the Roanoke settlers, including the harsh environment, strained relations with indigenous peoples, and logistical difficulties of transatlantic supply lines, highlight the precarious nature of these early colonial ventures. The failure of Roanoke stands in stark contrast to the eventual success of the Jamestown Colony, founded in 1607, which benefited from lessons learned from earlier attempts like Roanoke.

The mystery of the Roanoke Colony continues to captivate historians, archaeologists, and the general public, inspiring countless books, documentaries, and scholarly articles. Despite the wealth of research and speculation, the ultimate fate of the colonists remains elusive, a testament to the complexities and uncertainties of early colonial history. The unanswered questions surrounding Roanoke serve as a reminder of the challenges and risks faced by the first Europeans who ventured into the New World and the enduring mysteries that still linger from those formative years.

As research continues, new discoveries and technologies may eventually shed light on what happened to the lost colonists of Roanoke. For now, their story remains one of the great unsolved mysteries of American history, a compelling narrative that continues to intrigue and inspire those who seek to uncover the truth. The legacy of the Roanoke Colony endures as a symbol of both the promise and peril of early exploration and settlement in North America, and the enduring human fascination with the unknown.

Chapter 3: The Death of Alexander the Great

The death of Alexander the Great is a historical event shrouded in mystery and speculation, marked by its suddenness and the far-reaching consequences it had on the ancient world. Born in 356 BCE in Pella, the ancient capital of Macedonia, Alexander was the son of King Philip II and Queen Olympias. He ascended to the throne at the age of 20 after the assassination of his father and embarked on an unprecedented military campaign that expanded the Macedonian Empire across three continents, stretching from Greece to Egypt and as far as India. By the time of his death in 323 BCE at the age of 32, he had forged one of the largest empires in history. However, the circumstances surrounding his death have remained a topic of intense debate among historians, scholars, and biographers for over two millennia.

Alexander's death occurred in the city of Babylon, the heart of his newly acquired Persian Empire. Accounts of his final days are primarily derived from ancient historians such as Arrian, Plutarch, and Diodorus Siculus, though these sources often contradict one another and are influenced by the political and cultural biases of their time. According to these accounts, Alexander began showing signs of illness after a prolonged period of heavy drinking at a banquet celebrating his victories. Over the course of several days, his condition deteriorated rapidly, leading to high fever, severe abdominal pain, and ultimately his death on June 10 or 11, 323 BCE.

The rapid progression of Alexander's illness and his relatively young age have led to a plethora of theories regarding the cause of his death. One of the most widely accepted theories is that Alexander succumbed to a fever caused by an infectious disease such as malaria or typhoid. The ancient world was rife with diseases, and Alexander's extensive travels through various climates and terrains would have exposed him to numerous pathogens. Malaria, transmitted by mosquitoes, was common in the marshlands around Babylon, and typhoid fever, caused by contaminated food or water, was a frequent cause of mortality in ancient armies. Both diseases could account for the symptoms described in historical records, including the high fever, delirium, and gastrointestinal distress that Alexander experienced.

Another plausible explanation is that Alexander may have died from a condition known as acute pancreatitis, which can be triggered by excessive alcohol consumption and can cause severe abdominal pain, fever, and systemic inflammation. Alexander was known for his heavy drinking, and his symptoms are consistent with this diagnosis. However, the lack of precise medical knowledge in ancient times makes it difficult to definitively identify the cause of his illness based on the available historical accounts.

In addition to natural causes, there has long been speculation that Alexander may have been poisoned. This theory is fueled by the political intrigue and rivalries that surrounded him throughout his life. After his death, his empire was plunged into chaos, with his generals, known as the Diadochi, vying for power and control over different regions. Some ancient sources, such as Plutarch and Diodorus, suggest that Alexander's sudden death was the result of a conspiracy orchestrated by one or more of his close associates who feared his growing power and influence. Potential suspects include his half-brother Arrhidaeus, his general Antipater, and even his wife Roxana, all of whom had motives to see him removed from power.

The poisoning theory is supported by the fact that Alexander's symptoms developed over a relatively short period, which could be indicative of the effects of a toxic substance. However, there are significant challenges to this hypothesis. The exact poison used would need to have been one that caused a slow and progressive decline, allowing for the possibility of a prolonged agony, which fits some descriptions of Alexander's final days. Various poisons known to the ancient Greeks and Persians, such as hemlock or aconite, could cause such symptoms, but the logistics of administering the poison in a controlled and undetectable manner would have been complex.

Another intriguing possibility is that Alexander's death was the result of an autoimmune disorder such as Guillain-Barré Syndrome (GBS), which can cause paralysis and is often preceded by an infection. Some modern medical historians have suggested that Alexander's symptoms, including the high fever, pain, and eventual paralysis, could be consistent with GBS. This theory posits that a viral or bacterial infection triggered an immune response that led to his body's own immune system attacking his peripheral nervous system. However, this diagnosis is speculative and relies on interpreting ancient texts through the lens of modern medical understanding, which may not accurately reflect the reality of Alexander's condition.

Adding to the complexity of determining the cause of Alexander's death is the political and cultural context of his time. Alexander's conquests had created a vast and diverse empire that encompassed numerous peoples, languages, and traditions. His death left a power vacuum that led to the fracturing of his empire into several Hellenistic kingdoms ruled by his former generals. This fragmentation was marked by decades of warfare and instability, as the Diadochi fought for dominance and control over the territories that Alexander had united. The political turmoil that followed his death may have influenced contemporary and later accounts of his demise, with different factions seeking to justify their actions or undermine their rivals by attributing Alexander's death to foul play or divine retribution.

Furthermore, Alexander's own ambitions and personality may have contributed to the mystery surrounding his death. He was known for his relentless pursuit of glory and his belief in his own divinity, often portraying himself as a god-king in the tradition of the ancient Near Eastern rulers he conquered. This self-perception may have influenced the accounts of his death, with some sources suggesting that he believed he was invincible or protected by the gods. The sudden and unexplained nature of his death, therefore, may have been seen as a sign of divine will or a punishment for his hubris, adding a layer of myth and legend to the historical record.

The legacy of Alexander the Great's death extends beyond the immediate aftermath of his demise and the political struggles that ensued. His life and achievements have been the subject of extensive historical, literary, and artistic works, shaping the cultural and intellectual landscape of the ancient and modern worlds. The unresolved mystery of his death continues to captivate scholars and enthusiasts, serving as a reminder of the complexities and uncertainties that characterize historical events and the challenges of interpreting them through the lens of different perspectives and contexts.

In the centuries since Alexander's death, his story has been retold and reinterpreted in countless ways, reflecting the enduring fascination with his character and his accomplishments. The search for answers to the mystery of his death has inspired numerous theories and debates, highlighting the interplay between historical evidence, medical knowledge, and cultural narratives. As new discoveries and insights emerge, the story of Alexander's death continues to evolve, offering fresh perspectives on one of history's most enigmatic figures.

Ultimately, the death of Alexander the Great remains a testament to the enduring allure of historical mysteries and the complexity of human history. It serves as a reminder that even the most powerful and influential individuals are subject to the uncertainties of life and death, and that the quest for understanding and meaning is a timeless pursuit that transcends the ages. Whether Alexander's death was the result of natural causes, foul play, or divine intervention, it stands as a pivotal moment in history, marking the end of an era and the beginning of a new chapter in the story of human civilization.

Chapter 4: The Mysterious Demise of Tutankhamun

The mysterious demise of Tutankhamun, often referred to as King Tut, has intrigued historians, archaeologists, and the general public for nearly a century. Tutankhamun, a pharaoh of the 18th dynasty of ancient Egypt, ascended to the throne at a young age and ruled from approximately 1332 to 1323 BCE. His reign was relatively short and unremarkable compared to other pharaohs, but his tomb, discovered nearly intact in 1922 by British archaeologist Howard Carter, catapulted him to global fame. The circumstances surrounding his untimely death at around 19 years old have been the subject of extensive research and debate, with various theories proposed over the years to explain his premature demise.

Tutankhamun was born around 1341 BCE, during a tumultuous period in Egyptian history known as the Amarna Period. This era was marked by the religious revolution led by his predecessor, Akhenaten, who introduced the worship of a single deity, Aten, the sun disk, in place of the traditional Egyptian pantheon. This shift led to significant political and social upheaval. Tutankhamun, believed to be the son of Akhenaten and one of his sisters, ascended to the throne as a child, possibly as young as eight or nine, following Akhenaten's death and the brief reign of a successor, likely Smenkhkare or Neferneferuaten.

One of the most significant actions taken during Tutankhamun's reign was the restoration of the traditional polytheistic religion and the abandonment of the Aten cult. He moved the capital back to Thebes from Akhetaten (modern-day Amarna), reestablishing the worship of the gods Amun and others. These changes were likely orchestrated by powerful advisors and priests who sought to restore stability and traditional values to Egypt. Tutankhamun's reign, though brief, was marked by efforts to undo the radical changes of his father and restore the old order.

Despite his historical significance, much of the fascination with Tutankhamun centers on the discovery of his tomb in the Valley of the Kings in 1922. Howard Carter's excavation revealed a nearly intact burial chamber filled with treasures, artifacts, and the young pharaoh's mummy, providing unprecedented insight into ancient Egyptian culture and burial practices. The tomb's discovery was a sensation, capturing the world's imagination and leading to widespread interest in Egyptology. However, the intact nature of the tomb also raised questions about Tutankhamun's sudden death and the circumstances that led to his burial in such a relatively modest tomb for a pharaoh.

The exact cause of Tutankhamun's death has been a subject of debate and speculation since the discovery of his tomb. Initial theories ranged from murder to accidental injury to various diseases. Early examinations of his mummy, conducted by Carter and others, suggested possible foul play, with a fracture in the back of his skull leading some to speculate that he had been murdered, possibly by a blow to the head. This theory was supported by the turbulent political environment of the time, where power struggles and assassinations were not uncommon. However, later studies and modern imaging techniques have cast doubt on this hypothesis, suggesting that the skull fracture may have occurred post-mortem during the embalming process or as a result of damage to the mummy over time.

One of the most compelling theories regarding Tutankhamun's death is that he may have succumbed to complications from an injury, possibly a fracture in his left leg. In 1968, an X-ray examination revealed a break in Tutankhamun's femur, which had shown signs of infection. This finding led to the suggestion that the young pharaoh may have suffered a serious injury, possibly from a chariot accident or a fall, which became infected and ultimately proved fatal. Given the lack of modern medical treatments, even a relatively minor injury could have been life-threatening in ancient Egypt. In 2005, a team of Egyptian and international researchers conducted a CT scan of Tutankhamun's mummy, confirming the presence of a fracture and evidence of infection, supporting the theory that his death may have resulted from complications related to an injury.

Further complicating the investigation into Tutankhamun's death are the genetic and pathological analyses of his mummy, which have revealed a range of health issues that may have contributed to his early demise. In 2010, a team of researchers led by Zahi Hawass, then Secretary General of the Egyptian Supreme Council of Antiquities, conducted a comprehensive genetic study of Tutankhamun and his family. The study revealed that Tutankhamun suffered from several genetic disorders, including a cleft palate and a clubfoot, as well as a condition known as Kohler disease, which affects bone development. These findings suggest that the pharaoh may have been frail and in poor health for much of his life, making him more susceptible to illness and injury.

In addition to his physical ailments, genetic analysis also revealed that Tutankhamun was likely infected with multiple strains of malaria, a disease endemic to ancient Egypt. Malaria could have weakened his immune system and exacerbated any injuries or infections he sustained, contributing to his death. The combination of genetic disorders, physical frailty, and chronic illness paints a picture of a young ruler who was physically vulnerable and may have struggled with significant health challenges throughout his short life.

The political context of Tutankhamun's reign also provides potential clues to his death. As a child pharaoh, he would have been heavily influenced by his advisors and the powerful priesthood, who sought to restore the traditional religious practices that had been upended by his father, Akhenaten. Tutankhamun's sudden death and the subsequent power struggles among his advisors, including figures like Ay and Horemheb, who would go on to rule Egypt, suggest a period of significant political instability. While there is no concrete evidence to support the theory of foul play, the possibility that Tutankhamun's death was the result of political intrigue or assassination cannot be entirely ruled out, given the context of his reign and the ambitions of those around him.

The discovery of Tutankhamun's tomb and the examination of his mummy have also provided insights into the burial practices and beliefs of ancient Egypt. The lavish array of goods found in his tomb, including the iconic gold funerary mask, jewelry, weapons, and other artifacts, reflects the Egyptians' beliefs in the afterlife and the importance of ensuring that the deceased was well-equipped for their journey to the next world. The presence of such a wealth of items in Tutankhamun's tomb, despite his relatively minor status as a pharaoh, underscores the importance placed on the burial process and the belief in the pharaoh's divine status and role in maintaining cosmic order.

The condition of Tutankhamun's mummy and the artifacts found in his tomb also provide evidence of the embalming and mummification techniques used by the ancient Egyptians. The examination of his mummy revealed that the embalming process had been hastily performed, possibly due to the suddenness of his death or the need to prepare his body quickly for burial. The discovery of charred linen wrappings and signs of rushed mummification practices suggests that Tutankhamun's death may have caught his embalmers unprepared, leading to a less than perfect preservation of his body.

Despite the extensive research and numerous theories proposed over the years, the exact cause of Tutankhamun's death remains a mystery. The combination of injury, infection, genetic disorders, and chronic illness provides a plausible explanation for his premature demise, but the lack of definitive evidence means that we may never know the full story. The intrigue surrounding his death and the discovery of his tomb have ensured that Tutankhamun remains one of the most iconic and enigmatic figures in ancient history.

The fascination with Tutankhamun and the mystery of his death continues to captivate the public and inspire new research and exploration. Advances in technology, such as DNA analysis and imaging techniques, have provided new insights into his life and health, but have also raised new questions and challenges. As our understanding of ancient Egyptian history and culture evolves, so too does our perspective on the life and death of Tutankhamun, reflecting the enduring allure of one of history's most famous and mysterious figures. The story of Tutankhamun is a testament to the complexities of ancient history and the ongoing quest to uncover the secrets of the past, a journey that continues to captivate and inspire us today.

Chapter 5: The Enigmatic Passing of Marilyn Monroe

The enigmatic passing of Marilyn Monroe, a cultural icon whose life and death continue to captivate the world, remains one of the most enduring and controversial mysteries of the 20th century. Born Norma Jeane Mortenson on June 1, 1926, Monroe rose to unprecedented fame as an actress, model, and singer, becoming a symbol of glamour, beauty, and sexuality in the post-war era. Her untimely death on August 4, 1962, at the age of 36, officially ruled a probable suicide by overdose of barbiturates, has been the subject of widespread speculation, conspiracy theories, and debates for decades. The circumstances of her death, involving powerful figures, personal turmoil, and the dark underbelly of Hollywood, have led to numerous theories that challenge the official narrative and continue to intrigue those seeking to uncover the truth behind her tragic demise.

Marilyn Monroe's life was marked by both extraordinary success and profound personal struggles. Born to an unmarried mother, Gladys Pearl Baker, who battled mental illness, Monroe spent much of her childhood in foster homes and orphanages. Her early life was characterized by instability and abuse, experiences that left deep emotional scars. Despite these challenges, Monroe began a successful modeling career in her late teens, which eventually led to a contract with Twentieth Century Fox. Her early roles in films were minor, but her breakout came in 1950 with a series of performances that showcased her talent and magnetism, leading to starring roles in iconic films such as "Gentlemen Prefer Blondes," "Some Like It Hot," and "The Seven Year Itch."

Monroe's rise to fame was meteoric, and she quickly became one of the most famous and beloved actresses in Hollywood. Her on-screen persona of the glamorous and seductive blonde bombshell made her a cultural icon, but it also typecast her in roles that belied her desire for more serious acting challenges. Despite her public image as a confident and vivacious star, Monroe struggled with severe anxiety, depression, and substance abuse. Her personal life was tumultuous, marked by high-profile marriages to baseball legend Joe DiMaggio and playwright Arthur Miller, both of which ended in divorce. She also had numerous affairs and was rumored to have had relationships with several powerful and influential men, including President John F. Kennedy and his brother, Attorney General Robert F. Kennedy.

The final months of Monroe's life were marked by increasing instability and turmoil. She struggled with the pressures of fame, her deteriorating mental health, and a declining career. In early 1962, she was fired from the production of the film "Something's Got to Give" due to chronic absenteeism and erratic behavior, which further compounded her emotional distress and professional anxieties. Despite these challenges, she attempted to rebuild her career and personal life, making public appearances and rekindling relationships with influential figures in Hollywood and politics.

On the night of August 4, 1962, Monroe was found dead in her Brentwood home in Los Angeles. Her housekeeper, Eunice Murray, discovered her lifeless body in her bedroom, lying face down on her bed, with an empty bottle of barbiturates nearby. Monroe's physician, Dr. Ralph Greenson, and her internist, Dr. Hyman Engelberg, were called to the scene, and they pronounced her dead shortly after their arrival. The initial investigation by the Los Angeles Police Department concluded that Monroe's death was a probable suicide caused by an overdose of barbiturates. The autopsy, conducted by Dr. Thomas Noguchi, revealed that Monroe had ingested a lethal dose of the sedative Nembutal and the tranquilizer chloral hydrate, which combined to cause acute barbiturate poisoning. However, no pills or capsules were found in her stomach, suggesting that she may have ingested the drugs over a period of time rather than in a single, fatal dose.

The official ruling of Monroe's death as a probable suicide was based on her history of depression, substance abuse, and previous suicide attempts. However, this conclusion has been met with skepticism and controversy. Several inconsistencies and unexplained details surrounding the circumstances of her death have fueled speculation and conspiracy theories that challenge the official narrative. One of the most contentious aspects of Monroe's death is the timeline of events on the night she died. According to Murray, Monroe retired to her bedroom around 8:00 p.m. after speaking with her close friend, actor Peter Lawford, on the phone. Murray claimed that she became concerned when she noticed a light still on in Monroe's bedroom around midnight and was unable to get a response from her. She then contacted Monroe's psychiatrist, Dr. Greenson, who arrived and broke a window to gain access to the bedroom, discovering Monroe's body.

However, conflicting reports and testimonies have raised questions about the accuracy of this timeline. Some witnesses claimed that there was a delay in calling the police and that Monroe's body had been moved or repositioned before the authorities arrived. Additionally, there were discrepancies in the accounts of when Monroe was last seen alive and the exact time of her death. The presence of broken glass and the position of her body also raised suspicions of possible foul play.

Another significant area of controversy is the involvement of the Kennedys and the potential political implications of Monroe's death. Monroe's alleged affairs with President John F. Kennedy and Attorney General Robert F. Kennedy have long been the subject of speculation and rumor. Some theories suggest that Monroe's relationships with the Kennedys may have played a role in her death, either as a result of a deliberate cover-up or an accidental overdose orchestrated to silence her. Supporters of this theory argue that Monroe may have been privy to sensitive information or was perceived as a threat due to her connections with the Kennedys and other influential figures. These suspicions were fueled by reports of Robert F. Kennedy being in Los Angeles on the night of Monroe's death and the alleged presence of a mysterious "red diary" in which Monroe supposedly recorded details of her relationships and conversations with powerful men.

Further complicating the investigation are the numerous inconsistencies and anomalies in the autopsy report and the handling of Monroe's body. The toxicology report indicated lethal levels of barbiturates in her blood, but no residue was found in her stomach, leading some experts to question whether the drugs were ingested orally or administered through other means, such as injection or enema. Additionally, there were indications that Monroe had sustained bruises on her body, which were not adequately explained in the autopsy report. The lack of thorough forensic analysis and the possible tampering or destruction of evidence have led to suspicions that the true circumstances of Monroe's death were obscured or deliberately concealed.

Over the years, various individuals who were close to Monroe or involved in the investigation have come forward with conflicting accounts and claims that further muddle the narrative. Some have alleged that Monroe was the victim of a conspiracy involving powerful figures in Hollywood and politics, who sought to silence her or cover up her death to protect their reputations. Others suggest that Monroe's death was the result of a tragic accident or a cry for help that went unanswered. The involvement of figures such as Monroe's housekeeper, Eunice Murray, and her psychiatrist, Dr. Ralph Greenson, has also been scrutinized, with some questioning their roles and motivations in the events leading up to her death.

In addition to the speculation and conspiracy theories, Monroe's death has also been examined through the lens of her personal struggles and mental health issues. Monroe's life was marked by episodes of severe depression, anxiety, and substance abuse, which were exacerbated by the pressures of fame and the traumas of her early life. She had a history of seeking treatment for her mental health issues and had previously attempted suicide on multiple occasions. The combination of her emotional instability, addiction, and the tumultuous relationships in her life created a complex and precarious situation that may have contributed to her death.

The cultural impact of Marilyn Monroe's death extends far beyond the immediate aftermath of her passing. Monroe's life and legacy have been the subject of countless books, films, and academic studies, reflecting her enduring status as a cultural icon and symbol of the complexities and contradictions of celebrity. Her death has inspired ongoing fascination and debate, highlighting the interplay between fame, mental health, and the darker aspects of Hollywood and American society. The continued interest in Monroe's life and death underscores the public's enduring fascination with her as both a tragic figure and a symbol of beauty and glamour.

Despite the extensive research and numerous theories proposed over the years, the true circumstances of Marilyn Monroe's death remain a mystery. The combination of conflicting accounts, missing evidence, and the passage of time has made it difficult to reach a definitive conclusion about what happened on the night of August 4, 1962. The unresolved nature of her death and the various factors that may have contributed to it continue to fuel speculation and intrigue, ensuring that the story of Marilyn Monroe's enigmatic passing remains a topic of interest and debate for generations to come.

In the broader context of her life and legacy, Marilyn Monroe's death serves as a poignant reminder of the challenges and vulnerabilities faced by those who achieve extraordinary fame. Her story highlights the complexities of mental health, the pressures of public life, and the darker realities that can accompany the pursuit of success and recognition. Monroe's life and death continue to resonate with audiences around the world, reflecting the enduring allure and mystery of one of Hollywood's most iconic and tragic figures. As new research and perspectives emerge, the enigmatic passing of Marilyn Monroe remains a compelling and thought-provoking chapter in the history of American culture and the ongoing quest to understand the complexities of human experience.

Chapter 6: The Unsolved Murder of the Black Dahlia

The unsolved murder of the Black Dahlia is one of the most infamous and gruesome mysteries in American history. It remains a chilling enigma that has captivated public interest for over seven decades. The victim, Elizabeth Short, was a young woman with aspirations of becoming a Hollywood actress. Her brutal murder and the subsequent investigation have sparked countless theories, books, films, and ongoing speculation. The case not only highlights the dark underbelly of 1940s Los Angeles but also serves as a stark reminder of the brutal realities of crime and the often elusive nature of justice.

Elizabeth Short was born on July 29, 1924, in Boston, Massachusetts. She had a tumultuous childhood, marked by the early departure of her father, who abandoned the family when Elizabeth was just six years old. Raised by her mother, Phoebe Mae Short, Elizabeth moved frequently and spent much of her youth in various locations along the East Coast. Her striking beauty and dark hair earned her the nickname "Black Dahlia," a moniker that would later become synonymous with her tragic end. In pursuit of a career in Hollywood, Elizabeth relocated to Los Angeles, where she struggled to find work in the film industry and lived a transient lifestyle, often staying with friends or acquaintances.

On January 15, 1947, the mutilated body of Elizabeth Short was discovered in a vacant lot in the Leimert Park neighborhood of Los Angeles. Her body had been severed at the waist, drained of blood, and posed in a grotesque manner. The nature of her injuries was horrific; her face had been slashed from the corners of her mouth to her ears, creating a chilling "Glasgow smile." There were also signs of extensive torture, including cuts and bruises all over her body, and her internal organs had been removed. The body was found by Betty Bersinger, a local housewife who initially mistook it for a discarded mannequin. The discovery of Short's body set off a media frenzy, and her case quickly became known as the Black Dahlia murder.

The investigation into Elizabeth Short's murder was one of the largest and most intensive in the history of the Los Angeles Police Department (LAPD). Led by Chief of Detectives Thad Brown and Inspector Harry Hansen, the LAPD faced immense pressure from the public and media to solve the case. Despite numerous leads and a massive manhunt, the investigation was plagued by challenges from the start. The crime scene had been contaminated by curious onlookers and the media, who arrived before the police, making it difficult to gather evidence. Additionally, the lack of blood at the scene suggested that Short had been murdered elsewhere and her body transported and displayed post-mortem.

One of the most perplexing aspects of the Black Dahlia case was the sheer brutality of the crime. The dismemberment and mutilation of Elizabeth Short's body indicated a level of surgical precision and sadism that pointed to a killer with a deep-seated psychopathic nature. The autopsy, conducted by Dr. Frederick Newbarr, revealed that Short had been tortured and sexually assaulted before her death. The cause of death was determined to be a combination of hemorrhage from the facial lacerations and shock from the blows to the head.

The investigation into Elizabeth Short's murder produced a plethora of suspects, confessions, and leads, but no conclusive evidence or arrests. Over 150 suspects were interviewed, and countless individuals confessed to the crime, though most were quickly dismissed as attention-seekers or mentally unstable. The intense media coverage and public fascination with the case led to a flood of tips and false leads, further complicating the investigation. The LAPD explored connections to other unsolved murders, examined possible ties to organized crime, and scrutinized Short's acquaintances and personal life in an effort to uncover her killer.

One of the most significant suspects in the Black Dahlia case was Dr. George Hodel, a wealthy and influential physician in Los Angeles. Hodel came under suspicion after his son, Steve Hodel, a former LAPD detective, began investigating his father's past. Steve Hodel uncovered evidence that linked George Hodel to the crime, including photographs resembling Elizabeth Short found in his father's belongings and a series of incriminating audio recordings. In 1949, George Hodel was investigated by the LAPD in connection with the murder of his secretary, Ruth Spaulding, and was implicated in various other crimes, including medical malpractice and sexual abuse. Although the evidence against him was compelling, George Hodel was never formally charged in connection with the Black Dahlia murder, and he eventually fled to the Philippines, where he lived until his death in 1999.

Another prominent suspect was Leslie Dillon, a bellhop and aspiring writer with a disturbing fascination with crime. Dillon came to the attention of the LAPD after he wrote a series of letters to Dr. J. Paul de River, a police psychiatrist, detailing his interest in the Black Dahlia case and his belief that his friend, Jeff Connors, was the killer. During a series of interviews, Dillon provided detailed knowledge of the crime that had not been made public, leading police to suspect that he may have been involved. However, inconsistencies in his account and a lack of concrete evidence ultimately led to his release, and he was never formally charged.

Other suspects included Mark Hansen, a nightclub owner who knew Elizabeth Short and was reportedly one of the last people to see her alive, and Walter Bayley, a surgeon whose daughter was a close friend of Short's. Both men had plausible motives and connections to the case, but there was insufficient evidence to link either to the murder definitively. The investigation also explored possible ties to other unsolved murders, including those of Georgette Bauerdorf and Jeanne

French, who were both found dead under similar circumstances in the Los Angeles area around the same time.

The Black Dahlia case remains unsolved to this day, and the mystery surrounding Elizabeth Short's murder has spawned countless theories and speculation. Some believe that her death was the result of a personal vendetta or a crime of passion, while others suggest that she was the victim of a serial killer who may have been responsible for other unsolved murders in the area. The gruesome nature of the crime and the lack of conclusive evidence have led to widespread speculation that the killer was a skilled and calculating individual, possibly with medical or surgical training, who meticulously planned and executed the murder.

The legacy of the Black Dahlia case extends far beyond the details of Elizabeth Short's life and death. Her murder has become a symbol of the dark and often dangerous world of Hollywood and the vulnerability of those who seek fame and fortune in the entertainment industry. The case has inspired numerous books, films, and television shows, reflecting the enduring fascination with the mystery and the broader cultural themes it represents.

One of the most influential works inspired by the Black Dahlia case is James Ellroy's novel "The Black Dahlia," published in 1987. Ellroy's fictionalized account of the murder and the investigation captures the grim atmosphere of post-war Los Angeles and the pervasive sense of corruption and moral decay that characterized the city at the time. The novel explores the psychological and social factors that contributed to the crime, offering a dark and compelling portrait of a city and a culture grappling with the consequences of violence and ambition. The success of Ellroy's novel and its subsequent film adaptation have helped to keep the Black Dahlia case in the public eye and continue to inspire interest and speculation.

The Black Dahlia case has also had a significant impact on the field of criminal investigation and forensic science. The challenges faced by the LAPD in investigating Elizabeth Short's murder, including the contamination of the crime scene, the flood of false leads, and the difficulty in identifying viable suspects, highlight the complexities and limitations of criminal investigations. The case has prompted ongoing discussions about the importance of preserving evidence, the role of the media in shaping public perceptions of crime, and the need for advancements in forensic techniques and technology.

Despite the passage of time, the murder of Elizabeth Short continues to resonate as a powerful and haunting symbol of the darker aspects of human nature and the mysteries that can lie at the heart of even the most seemingly straightforward cases. The unanswered questions and enduring fascination with the Black Dahlia case serve as a reminder of the complexities and challenges of understanding and solving violent crimes and the ways in which the legacies of such cases can shape our understanding of justice, crime, and society.

As the years have passed, the Black Dahlia case has become a part of American folklore, a story that is retold and reinterpreted with each new generation. The enduring mystery of Elizabeth Short's murder and the fascination with her life and death reflect the broader human interest in the macabre and the unknown, as well as the ongoing quest for truth and justice. The case remains a poignant and chilling reminder of the unsolved mysteries that continue to captivate our imagination and challenge our understanding of the world around us.

Chapter 7: The Disappearance of Jimmy Hoffa

The disappearance of Jimmy Hoffa is one of the most enduring and intriguing mysteries of the 20th century, captivating the public and law enforcement alike with its complex web of organized crime, labor unions, and political intrigue. James Riddle Hoffa, known as Jimmy Hoffa, was a prominent American labor union leader who played a crucial role in the growth and success of the International Brotherhood of Teamsters (IBT). His sudden disappearance on July 30, 1975, has led to decades of speculation, investigation, and a plethora of conspiracy theories that continue to fascinate people to this day. The case remains officially unsolved, with Hoffa's fate shrouded in mystery despite extensive efforts to uncover the truth.

Jimmy Hoffa was born on February 14, 1913, in Brazil, Indiana. He grew up in a working-class family, and his early experiences with labor struggles and economic hardship deeply influenced his future career. Hoffa's father, a coal miner, died when Jimmy was seven, prompting the family to move to Detroit, Michigan, where Hoffa would later become a pivotal figure in the labor movement. Hoffa left school at the age of 14 to support his family, taking on various jobs that exposed him to the harsh realities of labor exploitation and the need for strong labor representation.

Hoffa's rise in the labor movement began in the 1930s when he became a local organizer for the Teamsters in Detroit. The Teamsters, a powerful labor union representing truck drivers and warehouse workers, were instrumental in negotiating better wages and working conditions for their members. Hoffa's charisma, determination, and shrewd negotiating skills quickly earned him a reputation as a formidable leader and advocate for workers' rights. By the late 1940s,

Hoffa had become a key figure in the national Teamsters organization, and in 1957, he was elected as the union's president.

Under Hoffa's leadership, the Teamsters grew into one of the most powerful and influential labor unions in the United States. Hoffa was known for his tenacity and willingness to use both legal and extralegal methods to achieve his goals, including negotiating with organized crime figures to secure better deals for his members. This close relationship with organized crime would later become a central element in the mystery of his disappearance. Hoffa's tenure as president of the Teamsters was marked by significant achievements, including the establishment of the National Master Freight Agreement, which standardized wages and working conditions for truck drivers across the country.

However, Hoffa's success also attracted the attention of law enforcement and government officials, who were increasingly concerned about his connections to organized crime and allegations of corruption within the Teamsters. In the 1960s, Hoffa became the target of intense scrutiny by the federal government, particularly from Attorney General Robert F. Kennedy, who was determined to bring him to justice. Hoffa was ultimately convicted of jury tampering, attempted bribery, and fraud in 1967 and was sentenced to 13 years in prison. Despite his imprisonment, Hoffa retained significant influence within the Teamsters and continued to fight for his release.

Hoffa was released from prison in 1971 after serving nearly five years of his sentence, thanks to a commutation from President Richard Nixon. The conditions of his release included a restriction that barred him from engaging in union activities until 1980, a stipulation that Hoffa was determined to challenge. Hoffa's efforts to regain control of the Teamsters and his persistent ambition to reclaim his position as union president set the stage for his mysterious disappearance.

On July 30, 1975, Jimmy Hoffa disappeared from the parking lot of the Machus Red Fox, a suburban Detroit restaurant. Hoffa had reportedly gone to the restaurant to meet with Anthony "Tony Jack" Giacalone, a Detroit Mafia captain, and Anthony "Tony Pro" Provenzano, a New Jersey Teamsters official with known Mafia connections. Hoffa was last seen waiting in the parking lot around 2:30 p.m., and he was never seen again. His car was found abandoned in the restaurant's parking lot later that evening, but there were no signs of a struggle or foul play. The disappearance of such a high-profile figure immediately sparked a massive investigation and media frenzy, with countless theories emerging about his fate.

The FBI quickly launched an extensive investigation into Hoffa's disappearance, operating under the code name "Hoffex." The investigation involved numerous interviews, wiretaps, and surveillance of known organized crime figures and associates of Hoffa. The prevailing theory was that Hoffa had been the victim of a mob hit, ordered by organized crime figures who saw him as a threat to their interests. Hoffa's attempts to regain control of the Teamsters and his knowledge of the union's illicit dealings with the Mafia made him a potential liability to powerful figures within both the labor movement and organized crime.

One of the key suspects in Hoffa's disappearance was Anthony "Tony Pro" Provenzano, a Teamsters official with strong Mafia ties who had a contentious relationship with Hoffa. Provenzano and Hoffa had reportedly had a falling out while Hoffa was in prison, and there were allegations that Provenzano had threatened Hoffa's life. Provenzano was in New Jersey at the time of Hoffa's disappearance and denied any involvement, but his known animosity towards Hoffa and his connections to organized crime made him a prime suspect in the case.

Another significant suspect was Anthony "Tony Jack" Giacalone, a Detroit Mafia captain who was allegedly scheduled to meet with Hoffa on the day of his disappearance. Giacalone had a long history of involvement in organized crime and was known to be an associate of Hoffa. Giacalone's role in the case has been the subject of much speculation, with some theories suggesting that he may have been involved in luring Hoffa to the meeting as part of a larger plot orchestrated by the Mafia.

Over the years, numerous individuals have come forward with claims and confessions related to Hoffa's disappearance, but none have provided conclusive evidence or led to the discovery of Hoffa's remains. One of the most notable confessions came from Frank "The Irishman" Sheeran, a former labor union official and mob enforcer, who claimed in his autobiography that he had been ordered by Mafia boss Russell Bufalino to kill Hoffa. According to Sheeran, he lured Hoffa to a house in Detroit and shot him before disposing of his body. Sheeran's account, while compelling, has been met with skepticism by some investigators and experts who question the accuracy of his claims and the lack of corroborating evidence.

In addition to Sheeran's confession, there have been numerous other theories about what happened to Hoffa and where his remains might be located. Some believe that Hoffa's body was disposed of in a remote area or buried in a secret location, while others speculate that his remains were incinerated or disposed of in a manner that would make them difficult to recover. Various locations, including abandoned properties, landfills, and construction sites, have been suggested as potential burial sites, leading to several high-profile searches and excavations over the years. One of the most infamous theories suggested that Hoffa's body was buried under the concrete at Giants Stadium in New Jersey, a claim that has been widely debunked but remains a popular element of the Hoffa legend.

Despite the extensive investigation and numerous theories, the case of Jimmy Hoffa's disappearance remains officially unsolved, and his fate continues to be a subject of fascination and speculation. The mystery of what happened to Hoffa has been the subject of countless books, documentaries, and films, including Martin Scorsese's "The Irishman," which explores Sheeran's confession and the broader context of Hoffa's disappearance. The case has become a part of American cultural folklore, symbolizing the intersection of organized crime, labor unions, and political intrigue.

The enduring mystery of Jimmy Hoffa's disappearance has also had a significant impact on the labor movement and the perception of labor unions in the United States. Hoffa's legacy as a labor leader who fought for workers' rights and improved conditions for millions of Teamsters members is often overshadowed by the controversies and criminal associations that marked his career. The case has highlighted the challenges of balancing labor advocacy with the influence of organized crime and the need for accountability and transparency within labor organizations.

The investigation into Hoffa's disappearance has continued for decades, with new leads and theories emerging periodically. The FBI has maintained an active case file on Hoffa, and law enforcement agencies have conducted several searches and excavations in an attempt to locate his remains. In 2013, the FBI conducted a search of a property in Oakland Township, Michigan, based on a tip from an informant who claimed to have knowledge of Hoffa's burial site. The search, like many others before it, yielded no evidence and served as a reminder of the challenges and complexities involved in solving such a high-profile and long-standing case.

The disappearance of Jimmy Hoffa remains one of the most enduring and compelling mysteries in American history. The case continues to capture the public's imagination and serves as a symbol of the dark intersections between labor, organized crime, and politics. The unresolved nature of Hoffa's fate and the myriad theories surrounding his disappearance ensure that his story will continue to be a topic of fascination and intrigue for generations to come. The legacy of Jimmy Hoffa, both as a labor leader and as a central figure in one of the most famous unsolved mysteries of the 20th century, underscores the enduring complexities of the human quest for justice and the persistent allure of the unknown.

Chapter 8: The Strange Death of Edgar Allan Poe

The strange and mysterious death of Edgar Allan Poe has intrigued and puzzled scholars, fans, and historians for more than a century and a half. Poe, a literary giant known for his macabre and gothic tales, lived a life as enigmatic as his works, and his demise only adds to his mystique. On October 7, 1849, Edgar Allan Poe died under circumstances that remain unclear and contentious to this day. The days leading up to his death are shrouded in ambiguity, conflicting reports, and a myriad of theories that continue to fuel debate and speculation.

Edgar Allan Poe was born on January 19, 1809, in Boston, Massachusetts. He was orphaned at a young age and taken in by John and Frances Allan of Richmond, Virginia. Poe's relationship with John Allan was tumultuous, marked by clashes over finances and Poe's pursuit of a literary career. Despite these challenges, Poe emerged as a pioneering and influential writer, known for his contributions to the genres of horror, detective fiction, and science fiction. His works, such as "The Raven," "The Tell-Tale Heart," and "The Fall of the House of Usher," have left an indelible mark on American literature and culture.

By the late 1840s, Poe's life had been marred by personal and professional struggles. He suffered from bouts of depression and alcoholism, exacerbated by the death of his wife, Virginia Clemm, in 1847. Despite these difficulties, Poe remained an active literary figure, giving lectures and working on new projects. In September 1849, Poe left Richmond, where he had been staying, with plans to travel to Philadelphia to finalize some business arrangements and then continue to New York. However, what happened next is a matter of considerable mystery and conjecture.

On September 28, 1849, Poe was found in a state of distress and disarray on the streets of Baltimore, Maryland, near Gunner's Hall, a public house and polling place for a local election. He was discovered by Joseph W. Walker, a typesetter, who noted that Poe was in dire need of immediate assistance. Walker sent a note to Dr. Joseph Snodgrass, a friend and acquaintance of Poe, describing his condition as "in great distress" and "in need of immediate assistance." Poe was taken to Washington College Hospital, where he remained for several days until his death on October 7, 1849, at the age of 40.

The exact circumstances of Poe's final days and the cause of his death are clouded in uncertainty. His medical records and death certificate have been lost, and the accounts of those who were with him in his final hours are often contradictory and incomplete. According to Dr. John Joseph Moran, the attending physician, Poe was never coherent enough to explain how he came to be in such a dire state, and his condition included delirium, hallucinations, and fits of unconsciousness. Moran's descriptions of Poe's symptoms have varied over the years, and his reliability as a source has been questioned due to inconsistencies and possible embellishments in his accounts.

Numerous theories have been proposed to explain Poe's death, ranging from plausible to outlandish. One of the earliest and most persistent theories is that Poe died as a result of alcoholism. Poe's struggles with alcohol are well-documented, and it is suggested that his intoxicated state led to his collapse and subsequent death. However, some of Poe's contemporaries, including his close friend John R. Thompson, disputed this theory, arguing that Poe had been abstaining from alcohol for a period before his death and that a small amount of alcohol could have had a disproportionately severe effect on him due to his low tolerance.

Another theory posits that Poe's death was the result of a practice known as "cooping," a form of voter fraud prevalent in 19th-century America. According to this theory, Poe was kidnapped by political operatives and forced to vote multiple times for a particular candidate in different disguises. Cooping often involved drugging or physically abusing the victim to prevent resistance or escape. Poe's disheveled appearance, unfamiliar clothing, and state of confusion when he was found lend some credence to this theory, suggesting he may have been a victim of such a scheme.

Other theories suggest that Poe's death was due to medical conditions such as epilepsy, diabetes, or even rabies. Dr. R. Michael Benitez, a cardiologist at the University of Maryland Medical Center, proposed in 1996 that Poe's symptoms matched those of rabies, including fever, confusion, and difficulty swallowing. This theory, while plausible, lacks concrete evidence, as no medical records or eyewitness accounts definitively confirm a rabies diagnosis. Similarly, epilepsy has been suggested based on Poe's reported history of seizures and possible genetic predisposition, but this remains speculative without corroborative evidence.

There are also theories that Poe was murdered or died as a result of foul play. Some suggest that he was targeted by enemies or rival writers who sought to harm him due to professional jealousy or personal grudges. Others believe that Poe was attacked by muggers or criminals and succumbed to his injuries. These theories are largely speculative and lack substantial evidence, but they reflect the persistent fascination with the idea of a sinister or violent end for the enigmatic author.

A more recent theory suggests that Poe's death was the result of carbon monoxide poisoning from coal gas, which was commonly used for indoor lighting in the 19th century. This theory, proposed by public health expert Albert Donnay in 1999, is based on the idea that chronic exposure to coal gas could have caused a range of symptoms, including confusion, hallucinations, and respiratory distress. However, this theory is difficult to prove, given the lack of available medical data from Poe's time.

In addition to these theories, some researchers have explored the possibility that Poe suffered from a brain tumor or other neurological condition that could have caused his erratic behavior and physical decline. In 2000, an analysis of Poe's hair conducted by Dr. R. Michael Benitez and Dr. John F. Codman suggested the presence of high levels of heavy metals, potentially indicating exposure to toxic substances or a medical condition affecting his brain. However, this theory, like many others, remains speculative and lacks definitive evidence.

The mystery of Edgar Allan Poe's death is compounded by the complex and often contradictory nature of the available evidence. The loss of Poe's medical records, the unreliability of contemporary accounts, and the passage of time have all contributed to the persistence of uncertainty surrounding his final days. The variety of theories reflects the multifaceted and enigmatic nature of Poe himself, whose life and works continue to captivate and confound.

Poe's death has had a profound impact on his legacy and the perception of his work. His macabre and mysterious demise has added to the allure and mystique of his literary persona, and his life and death have become the subject of countless books, articles, and artistic interpretations. The enduring fascination with Poe's death mirrors the themes of ambiguity, mortality, and the unknown that permeate his writing, reinforcing his status as a central figure in American literature and culture.

In the years following his death, Poe's reputation underwent significant transformation. Initially, his literary achievements were overshadowed by a campaign of character assassination led by his literary executor, Rufus Wilmot Griswold, who portrayed Poe as a drunken, deranged madman. This portrayal, while sensational and widely accepted at the time, has since been challenged and revised by scholars who recognize Poe's contributions to literature and his complex, multifaceted character.

Today, Edgar Allan Poe is celebrated as a master of gothic fiction and a pioneer of the modern detective story. His works have influenced countless writers and artists and continue to resonate with readers around the world. The mystery of his death, while unresolved, serves as a testament to the enduring power of his legacy and the timeless appeal of his dark, imaginative vision.

Chapter 9: The Unexplained Demise of Bruce Lee

The unexplained demise of Bruce Lee remains one of the most enigmatic and debated events in the history of martial arts and cinema. Bruce Lee, renowned for his revolutionary martial arts techniques, charismatic screen presence, and philosophical insights, was a cultural icon whose sudden death at the age of 32 shocked the world. Lee's death on July 20, 1973, was unexpected and has been the subject of extensive speculation, numerous conspiracy theories, and ongoing investigation, casting a shadow over his legacy and leaving unanswered questions that continue to intrigue fans and scholars.

Bruce Lee, born Lee Jun-fan on November 27, 1940, in San Francisco, California, to Chinese parents, spent his early years in Hong Kong, where he began studying martial arts under the tutelage of Yip Man, a master of Wing Chun. Lee's family moved back to the United States when he was 18, and he eventually settled in Seattle, Washington, where he attended the University of Washington. It was in the U.S. that Lee began to develop his own approach to martial arts, blending various styles and philosophies into a system he called Jeet Kune Do, or "The Way of the Intercepting Fist."

Lee's martial arts philosophy emphasized practicality, efficiency, and adaptability, challenging traditional notions of rigid styles and forms. He opened martial arts schools, taught students from diverse backgrounds, and began to make a name for himself as a martial arts innovator. His charismatic persona and exceptional physical abilities caught the attention of Hollywood, leading to roles in television and film, including the iconic TV series "The Green Hornet" and his breakthrough role in the movie "Enter the Dragon," which was released posthumously.

By the early 1970s, Bruce Lee had become a global superstar, celebrated not only for his martial arts prowess but also for his philosophical insights and cultural impact. His sudden death in 1973, just days before the release of "Enter the Dragon," left fans and the public in shock and disbelief. The official cause of death, as reported by the Hong Kong coroner, was cerebral edema, or swelling of the brain, attributed to an allergic reaction to the painkiller Equagesic. However, the lack of conclusive evidence and the unusual circumstances surrounding his death have led to a multitude of theories and ongoing speculation.

The events leading up to Bruce Lee's death are shrouded in ambiguity and conflicting accounts. On the day of his death, Lee was in Hong Kong working on pre-production for his next film, "Game of Death." He had met with his producer, Raymond Chow, and then visited the apartment of Taiwanese actress Betty Ting Pei to discuss her role in the film. According to Chow and Ting Pei, Lee complained of a headache and was given Equagesic, a common painkiller. He went to lie down to rest and never regained consciousness. Attempts to revive him were unsuccessful, and he was pronounced dead upon arrival at Queen Elizabeth Hospital in Hong Kong.

The official autopsy report concluded that Lee's death was due to a hypersensitivity to the painkiller, leading to cerebral edema. However, this explanation has been met with skepticism and criticism from various quarters. Critics argue that it is highly unusual for an individual to suffer a fatal reaction to a medication like Equagesic, which Lee had reportedly taken before without incident. The ambiguity of the official explanation, combined with Lee's status as a larger-than-life figure, has fueled a wide range of alternative theories and conjectures.

One of the most prominent theories suggests that Bruce Lee's death was the result of foul play, possibly orchestrated by organized crime figures or business rivals. Lee's success and influence in the martial arts world and the film industry had earned him both admirers and enemies. Some speculate that his refusal to adhere to traditional martial arts hierarchies and his efforts to introduce Chinese martial arts to a global audience may have angered influential figures, leading to a plot to eliminate him. However, there is little concrete evidence to support these claims, and they remain largely in the realm of conspiracy theory.

Another theory posits that Lee's death was the result of a delayed reaction to a previous injury or medical condition. In May 1973, just two months before his death, Lee had collapsed during a dubbing session for "Enter the Dragon" and was hospitalized for several days. At that time, he was diagnosed with cerebral edema, which was successfully treated. Some believe that this incident was a warning sign of an underlying medical issue that may have contributed to his death. However, the exact nature of this condition and its possible connection to his subsequent demise remains unclear.

One of the more controversial theories is that Bruce Lee's death was the result of drug use or an overdose. This theory has been fueled by reports of Lee's alleged use of cannabis and other substances to manage pain and enhance his training regimen. Some sources suggest that Lee may have taken a combination of drugs that led to a fatal reaction. However, toxicology reports from the time did not indicate the presence of any illegal drugs in his system, and this theory is disputed by those close to Lee, who maintain that he was not involved in substance abuse.

Another perspective is that Lee's death was the result of extreme physical exertion and the toll it took on his body. Lee was known for his rigorous training regimen, which included intense physical workouts, strict dietary practices, and a relentless pursuit of physical perfection. Some believe that his body may have been pushed to its limits, leading to complications such as heat stroke or electrolyte imbalance. Lee's widow, Linda Lee Cadwell, has suggested that his death may have been due to hypersensitivity to a substance in the medication he took, possibly exacerbated by his physical condition at the time.

In recent years, some researchers have explored the possibility that Bruce Lee's death was related to an underlying medical condition such as epilepsy or an undiagnosed congenital disorder. One theory suggests that Lee may have suffered from a condition known as hyperthermia, in which the body's ability to regulate its temperature is impaired, leading to overheating and potential complications such as cerebral edema. This theory is based on reports of Lee's sensitivity to heat and his use of dietary supplements that may have affected his body's thermoregulation. However, this remains speculative and lacks definitive evidence.

The mysterious circumstances of Bruce Lee's death have also given rise to various supernatural and metaphysical theories. Some believe that Lee was the victim of a curse, possibly linked to his family or his involvement in martial arts. This theory is often tied to the subsequent tragic death of his son, Brandon Lee, who died in a freak accident on the set of the film "The Crow" in 1993. The idea of a curse has been popularized by media and folklore, but it is generally regarded as a cultural myth rather than a plausible explanation.

The unexplained demise of Bruce Lee continues to captivate and intrigue people around the world. His death, much like his life, is enveloped in an aura of mystery and speculation that reflects his enduring legacy as a cultural icon and martial arts legend. Despite the passage of time and the efforts of investigators, the true cause of Bruce Lee's death remains elusive, and the numerous theories and conjectures surrounding it only add to the mystique that surrounds his name.

Bruce Lee's impact on martial arts, cinema, and popular culture is profound and far-reaching. His philosophy of self-expression, personal freedom, and the integration of martial arts techniques has inspired generations of practitioners and fans. His films, characterized by their dynamic fight choreography and powerful performances, have become classics of the genre, influencing countless filmmakers and actors. Lee's legacy as a trailblazer and visionary continues to resonate, and his untimely death has only served to amplify the legend that surrounds him.

In the decades since his passing, Bruce Lee has become a symbol of strength, determination, and cultural pride. His life and work have been the subject of numerous books, documentaries, and academic studies, each exploring different aspects of his philosophy, achievements, and the enduring mystery of his death. The fascination with Lee's life and the unanswered questions surrounding his demise ensure that he will remain a figure of enduring interest and inspiration.

The enigma of Bruce Lee's death serves as a reminder of the fragility of life and the complexities of the human body. Despite his extraordinary physical prowess and philosophical insights, Lee was ultimately mortal, subject to the same vulnerabilities and uncertainties as anyone else. The unresolved nature of his death invites reflection on the limits of human understanding and the mysteries that continue to challenge our quest for knowledge and truth.

As we continue to explore and celebrate the life and legacy of Bruce Lee, the mystery of his death remains a poignant and powerful element of his story. It is a testament to the enduring power of his influence and the fascination he continues to hold for people around the world. The unanswered questions and ongoing speculation surrounding his demise ensure that Bruce Lee will forever be remembered not only as a martial arts master and cultural icon but also as a figure whose life and death embody the profound and enduring mysteries of the human experience.

Chapter 10: The Mystery of the Mary Celeste

The Mary Celeste, often shrouded in an air of mystery, has intrigued maritime historians and enthusiasts for over a century. This American merchant brigantine was discovered adrift in the Atlantic Ocean on December 4, 1872, by the Canadian brigantine Dei Gratia. What makes the Mary Celeste a subject of enduring fascination is not merely its abandonment but the perplexing circumstances under which it was found. The ship was in seaworthy condition, with its cargo of denatured alcohol largely intact, and the crew's personal belongings undisturbed. However, there was no sign of the crew, the lifeboat was missing, and the ship's logbook stopped abruptly ten days before its discovery, leaving a void filled with speculation and conjecture.

The Mary Celeste set sail from New York City on November 7, 1872, bound for Genoa, Italy, under the command of Captain Benjamin Briggs. A seasoned and respected mariner, Briggs was accompanied by his wife, Sarah, their two-year-old daughter, Sophia, and a crew of seven. The ship was last seen on November 25, off the Azores, before its discovery adrift. Upon boarding the vessel, the crew of the Dei Gratia noted several curious details: the ship's clock was not functioning, the compass was destroyed, and a significant but not catastrophic amount of water was found between decks. Despite these anomalies, the ship was in sound condition to sail, ruling out a catastrophic event such as a sudden storm or collision as the immediate cause of abandonment.

Various theories have been proposed to explain the fate of the Mary Celeste's crew, each more intriguing than the last. One of the earliest and most widely accepted theories suggests that the crew abandoned ship in a hurry due to the fear of an imminent explosion. This theory posits that the denatured alcohol in the cargo hold might have started leaking, producing potentially flammable fumes. A small explosion or sudden increase in temperature could have panicked the crew into evacuating the ship prematurely. However, this theory does not fully explain why the crew, presumably in a lifeboat, was never found or why they would not return once the immediate danger had passed.

Another popular hypothesis involves foul play, including mutiny, piracy, or even insurance fraud. Some suggest that the crew might have been overcome by pirates, although this seems less likely given the absence of violence or theft aboard the ship. The insurance fraud theory implicates Captain Briggs in a scheme to fake the ship's disappearance for financial gain, though this is inconsistent with his character and the lack of evidence supporting such a plan.

Natural phenomena have also been considered. The possibility of a waterspout—a powerful tornado at sea—might explain the sudden and mysterious abandonment. Waterspouts could cause a sudden drop in pressure, which might explain why the crew would hastily abandon the vessel, fearing it was about to capsize. However, this still fails to account for the crew's complete disappearance. Another natural explanation involves the potential for a seaquake or underwater earthquake, which could have induced a sudden and inexplicable fear of sinking, prompting an emergency evacuation.

The role of human error cannot be discounted. Perhaps Captain Briggs miscalculated a navigational hazard, or an unforeseen medical emergency necessitated abandoning ship. Given the era's limited communication technology and the isolation of transatlantic voyages, such an emergency could have precipitated a series of decisions that ultimately led to the crew's disappearance.

Some theories delve into the realm of the supernatural. The Bermuda Triangle, despite its geographical irrelevance to the actual location of the Mary Celeste, has been invoked by those favoring paranormal explanations. Similarly, ghost ship legends and sea monster myths contribute to the vessel's enigmatic narrative. These supernatural speculations, while captivating, often lack the empirical support needed to be taken seriously by historians and scientists.

One often overlooked aspect of the Mary Celeste mystery is the psychological state of its crew. Long voyages in confined spaces could lead to paranoia, mutiny, or mental breakdowns. The isolation and monotony of sea life, coupled with the ever-present dangers of maritime travel, might have triggered a collective or individual decision to abandon ship, particularly if compounded by other stressors like bad weather or illness.

The story of the Mary Celeste has been further complicated by fictional accounts and sensationalist journalism. Sir Arthur Conan Doyle, the creator of Sherlock Holmes, wrote a short story titled "J. Habakuk Jephson's Statement" in 1884, which fictionalized the ship's mystery and introduced elements like sea monsters and African tribes, fueling public fascination and misinformation. The blending of fact and fiction has made it difficult to separate genuine evidence from creative embellishment.

The maritime inquiry conducted by the British Admiralty in Gibraltar, where the Dei Gratia brought the Mary Celeste, concluded with no definitive answers. Despite extensive investigations, including interviews with the crew of the Dei Gratia and examination of the Mary Celeste herself, the mystery remained unresolved. The lack of conclusive evidence has left the door open to endless speculation and has cemented the Mary Celeste's place in maritime lore.

Over the years, numerous expeditions and modern technologies, including underwater archaeology and advanced forensic methods, have attempted to shed light on the mystery. Despite these efforts, the fate of the Mary Celeste's crew remains one of the most compelling unsolved mysteries in nautical history. The ship itself continued to sail under various owners until it met its final end, deliberately wrecked off the coast of Haiti in 1885 in an attempt at insurance fraud.

The enduring legacy of the Mary Celeste lies not only in the enigma of its abandoned crew but also in its representation of the unknown perils of the sea. It serves as a poignant reminder of the inherent dangers of maritime travel in the 19th century and the thin line between safety and disaster. The case of the Mary Celeste continues to captivate the imagination, inspiring books, films, and scholarly articles, each exploring the myriad possibilities behind this timeless maritime mystery.

Chapter 11: The Death of Princess Diana

The death of Princess Diana, Princess of Wales, remains one of the most shocking and controversial events of the late 20th century. On August 31, 1997, the world awoke to the devastating news that Diana, along with her companion Dodi Fayed and their driver Henri Paul, had died in a car crash in the Pont de l'Alma tunnel in Paris, France. Her sudden and tragic death sent shockwaves across the globe, leaving millions mourning the loss of the "People's Princess," a beloved public figure known for her humanitarian efforts, grace, and candidness.

Diana Frances Spencer was born on July 1, 1961, and rose to fame when she married Charles, Prince of Wales, in 1981. Their wedding was a global event, watched by millions. However, behind the fairy tale façade, Diana's life was fraught with personal struggles, including a tumultuous marriage plagued by infidelity and intense media scrutiny. Despite these challenges, Diana dedicated herself to various charitable causes, such as AIDS awareness, landmine clearance, and advocating for the homeless and mentally ill, earning widespread admiration and affection.

The events leading up to Diana's death began on the evening of August 30, 1997. Diana and Dodi Fayed, son of Egyptian billionaire Mohamed Al-Fayed, had spent the summer together, traveling aboard Mohamed Al-Fayed's yacht and staying at his residence in Paris. That night, they dined at the Ritz Hotel, owned by Mohamed Al-Fayed, before deciding to leave for Dodi's apartment in the early hours of August 31. To avoid paparazzi, a decoy vehicle was sent out from the front of the hotel while Diana, Dodi, their bodyguard Trevor Rees-Jones, and driver Henri Paul left from the rear entrance.

As they sped away from the hotel, they were pursued by paparazzi on motorcycles. Henri Paul, the driver, was later found to have a high blood alcohol level, raising questions about his fitness to drive. The car, a Mercedes-Benz S280, entered the Pont de l'Alma tunnel at high speed, estimated to be around 65 mph, more than twice the tunnel's speed limit. Paul lost control of the vehicle, which collided with a pillar inside the tunnel. Dodi Fayed and Henri Paul died instantly, while Diana was critically injured. Trevor Rees-Jones, the bodyguard, was the only survivor, albeit with severe injuries.

Emergency services arrived quickly, and Diana was transported to the Pitié-Salpêtrière Hospital. Despite extensive efforts to save her, including heart massage and internal cardiac massage, Diana succumbed to her injuries at 4:00 a.m. local time. The cause of death was later determined to be internal bleeding resulting from a ruptured pulmonary vein.

The immediate aftermath of Diana's death saw an unprecedented outpouring of grief. Mourners gathered outside Buckingham Palace, Kensington Palace, and the site of the crash in Paris, leaving flowers, candles, and heartfelt messages. Diana's funeral, held on September 6, 1997, at Westminster Abbey, was watched by an estimated 2.5 billion people worldwide. Her sons, Prince William and Prince Harry, walked behind her coffin in a poignant display of sorrow and resilience.

Despite the initial determination that Diana's death was an accident, fueled by the reckless driving of Henri Paul and the paparazzi chase, numerous conspiracy theories emerged, suggesting foul play. Mohamed Al-Fayed, in particular, was vocal in his belief that the crash was not an accident but rather a result of a conspiracy orchestrated by the British establishment, including the royal family and security services. He posited that Diana and Dodi were murdered to prevent them from marrying and having a child, which he claimed would be unacceptable to the British monarchy.

In response to these allegations and the ongoing public interest, the British Metropolitan Police launched Operation Paget in 2004, a comprehensive inquiry into the conspiracy theories surrounding Diana's death. After three years of investigation, the report, published in 2007, found no evidence of conspiracy and concluded that Diana's death was a tragic accident, primarily caused by the grossly negligent driving of Henri Paul and the relentless pursuit by the paparazzi.

The French authorities also conducted their investigation, which corroborated the findings of Operation Paget. They confirmed that Henri Paul was under the influence of alcohol and prescription drugs at the time of the crash, impairing his judgment and ability to drive safely. The vehicle's excessive speed and the failure of the occupants to wear seat belts were also cited as contributing factors.

Despite these official conclusions, speculation and alternative theories persist. Some suggest that the bright flash of light reported by witnesses just before the crash was a deliberate attempt to blind the driver. Others question the actions and motives of the paparazzi, suggesting that they may have played a more direct role in the crash. Additionally, there are claims of tampered evidence and cover-ups, further fueling suspicion and mistrust.

Princess Diana's legacy continues to resonate today, not only through her humanitarian work but also through her sons, Prince William and Prince Harry, who have carried forward her charitable endeavors and commitment to public service. Her life and untimely death have been the subject of numerous books, documentaries, and films, reflecting the enduring fascination with her story and the broader implications of her tragic demise.

Diana's death also had a significant impact on the British monarchy, prompting a reevaluation of its relationship with the media and the public. The initial response of the royal family to Diana's death was criticized as being aloof and out of touch with the public's grief, leading to a rare televised address by Queen Elizabeth II, in which she paid tribute to Diana and acknowledged the widespread mourning. This moment marked a shift towards a more modern and accessible monarchy, more attuned to the sentiments of the people.

In the years since her death, Diana's influence on fashion, philanthropy, and the public perception of the royal family has remained profound. She is remembered not only for her style and grace but also for her compassion and determination to use her platform to effect positive change. The memorials and charities established in her name continue to honor her legacy, ensuring that the "People's Princess" is never forgotten.

The death of Princess Diana remains a complex and emotive subject, interwoven with themes of tragedy, conspiracy, and enduring public fascination. While official investigations have provided plausible explanations for the circumstances surrounding her death, the aura of mystery and speculation persists, reflecting the deep impact she had on the world and the unresolved questions that continue to intrigue and inspire debate.

Chapter 12: The Assassination of John F. Kennedy

The assassination of John F. Kennedy, the 35th President of the United States, on November 22, 1963, remains one of the most profoundly impactful and controversially debated events in American history. Kennedy was shot while riding in a motorcade through Dealey Plaza in Dallas, Texas. His death shocked the nation and the world, leading to an outpouring of grief and a series of investigations and conspiracy theories that continue to fuel speculation decades later.

On that fateful day, President Kennedy was in Dallas as part of a political trip to Texas, aimed at mending political fences among Democratic factions and garnering support for his reelection campaign. He was accompanied by his wife, Jacqueline Kennedy, Texas Governor John Connally, and Connally's wife, Nellie. The motorcade route had been publicized in advance, and large crowds lined the streets to catch a glimpse of the charismatic leader and his stylish wife.

At approximately 12:30 p.m., as the motorcade passed the Texas School Book Depository, shots rang out. Kennedy was struck by two bullets, one in the upper back and one in the head. Governor Connally was also wounded. The presidential limousine sped to Parkland Memorial Hospital, but Kennedy's injuries were too severe, and he was pronounced dead at 1:00 p.m. Central Standard Time. The news was broadcast to a stunned nation by CBS anchor Walter Cronkite, cementing a moment of collective trauma in American consciousness.

In the immediate aftermath, law enforcement agencies scrambled to identify and apprehend the assassin. Within hours, Lee Harvey Oswald, an employee at the Texas School Book Depository, was arrested. Oswald, a former Marine who had briefly defected to the Soviet Union, denied shooting anyone, claiming he was a patsy. Two days later, while being transferred to a more secure jail, Oswald was shot and killed by nightclub owner Jack Ruby in a moment captured on live television, adding another layer of complexity and conspiracy to the already shocking events.

President Kennedy's assassination prompted the formation of the Warren Commission, chaired by Chief Justice Earl Warren, to investigate the circumstances of the murder. The Commission's report, published in September 1964, concluded that Lee Harvey Oswald acted alone in assassinating Kennedy and that there was no evidence of a conspiracy. This conclusion was based on ballistic evidence, eyewitness testimony, and forensic analysis, including the infamous "single bullet theory" that posited one bullet caused multiple wounds to both Kennedy and Connally.

Despite the Warren Commission's findings, doubts and alternative theories began to emerge almost immediately. Critics argued that the Commission failed to thoroughly investigate all possible leads and dismissed crucial evidence. Eyewitnesses in Dealey Plaza reported hearing shots from the grassy knoll, an area to the front and right of the motorcade, suggesting the possibility of multiple shooters. The acoustical evidence from police radio transmissions analyzed years later seemed to indicate multiple gunshots, further fueling speculation.

Several other investigations followed, including the House Select Committee on Assassinations (HSCA) in the late 1970s. The HSCA concluded that there was a high probability of a conspiracy, based on acoustical evidence indicating the presence of a second gunman. However, the Committee could not identify any individual or group responsible and upheld that Oswald fired the fatal shots. This conclusion only added to the plethora of theories and suspicions surrounding the assassination.

Various conspiracy theories have implicated a wide range of potential perpetrators, including the Mafia, anti-Castro Cuban exiles, the Soviet Union, the CIA, the FBI, and even elements within the U.S. government itself. The Mafia theory posits that organized crime figures orchestrated the assassination in retaliation for the Kennedy administration's crackdown on organized crime, spearheaded by Attorney General Robert Kennedy. The anti-Castro Cuban theory suggests that militant Cuban exiles, angered by Kennedy's perceived betrayal during the Bay of Pigs invasion and subsequent handling of the Cuban Missile Crisis, sought revenge.

Another theory implicates the Soviet Union or Cuban intelligence agencies, motivated by Cold War tensions and the administration's aggressive anti-communist stance. The CIA and FBI theories revolve around the notion that rogue elements within these agencies, dissatisfied with Kennedy's policies and fearing his potential rapprochement with the Soviet Union, orchestrated the assassination to prevent a shift in U.S. foreign policy.

The lack of definitive evidence and the complexity of the case have kept these theories alive, bolstered by numerous books, films, and documentaries exploring different angles and uncovering new information. Oliver Stone's 1991 film "JFK," based on New Orleans District Attorney Jim Garrison's investigation, popularized the idea of a vast conspiracy and criticized the Warren Commission's findings, contributing to renewed public interest and skepticism.

In addition to conspiracy theories, numerous discrepancies and unanswered questions about the official narrative have fueled ongoing debate. For example, the handling and autopsy of Kennedy's body were marred by procedural irregularities and conflicting reports from medical personnel. The Zapruder film, a key piece of visual evidence capturing the assassination, has been scrutinized frame by frame, with differing interpretations of the events depicted.

The role of the Secret Service and the security measures taken on the day of the assassination have also been questioned. Some critics argue that security lapses allowed the assassination to occur and that the Secret Service's actions immediately following the shooting were inadequate or suspicious. The rapidity of Oswald's arrest and subsequent murder by Jack Ruby have raised suspicions of a cover-up, with Ruby's motives and connections remaining a topic of intrigue.

The impact of Kennedy's assassination on American society and politics was profound. It marked the end of a brief era of optimism and idealism known as "Camelot" and ushered in a period of political turmoil and distrust. Lyndon B. Johnson, who was sworn in as President aboard Air Force One just hours after Kennedy's death, inherited a nation in mourning and faced significant challenges, including escalating involvement in Vietnam and the civil rights movement.

Kennedy's death also had lasting effects on U.S. security protocols and the Secret Service's protective measures. The assassination highlighted the vulnerabilities of presidential security, leading to significant changes in the way the Secret Service operates and the implementation of more stringent security protocols for future presidents.

In the decades since Kennedy's assassination, numerous government documents have been declassified, providing new insights but also raising additional questions. The release of these documents, mandated by the President John F. Kennedy Assassination Records Collection Act of 1992, has been sporadic, and some remain classified for national security reasons. The continued withholding of certain documents has perpetuated suspicions of a cover-up and the belief that the full truth has yet to be revealed.

The assassination of John F. Kennedy remains a defining moment in American history, emblematic of a broader era of upheaval and change. It has left an indelible mark on the national psyche, symbolizing the fragility of political leadership and the enduring quest for truth and justice. The myriad theories and unresolved questions surrounding the event reflect a deep-seated need to understand and make sense of a tragedy that fundamentally altered the course of the nation.

Kennedy's legacy, shaped by his inspiring rhetoric, visionary policies, and tragic death, continues to influence contemporary politics and culture. His calls for public service, space exploration, and civil rights remain relevant, inspiring new generations to engage in public life and pursue a better future. The unresolved nature of his assassination, however, serves as a reminder of the complexities and uncertainties inherent in historical events, challenging us to critically examine the past and seek truth amidst ambiguity.

Chapter 13: The Mysterious Death of Rasputin

The mysterious death of Grigori Rasputin, the enigmatic Russian mystic and confidant to the Romanov family, is a tale shrouded in intrigue, conspiracy, and legend. Rasputin, born on January 21, 1869, in a small village in Siberia, rose to prominence in the early 20th century as a trusted advisor to Tsar Nicholas II and his wife, Tsarina Alexandra. His influence over the Russian royal family, particularly his purported healing abilities and spiritual guidance, made him a controversial and polarizing figure, both within the court and among the Russian populace.

Rasputin's journey to power began in his early adulthood when he left his family and embarked on a pilgrimage across Russia and beyond. During these travels, he gained a reputation as a holy man with healing powers and prophetic abilities. His charisma and persuasive personality earned him a following, and by 1905, he had made his way to St. Petersburg, the heart of Russian political and social life. It was here that Rasputin's life intersected with the Romanovs.

The Romanov family, particularly Tsarina Alexandra, were deeply religious and believed in mysticism. They were desperate for a solution to their son Alexei's hemophilia, a genetic disorder that caused severe bleeding and threatened the young heir's life. Rasputin's apparent ability to alleviate Alexei's suffering through prayer and unconventional methods endeared him to Alexandra, who believed he was a divine healer sent by God to save her son and, by extension, the Russian monarchy.

Rasputin's influence over the royal family grew, leading to his involvement in state affairs. This unprecedented access and sway over the Tsar and Tsarina alarmed many in the Russian aristocracy, clergy, and political circles. They viewed Rasputin as a charlatan and a threat to the stability of the Russian Empire. Rumors of his debauchery, including allegations of excessive drinking, womanizing, and corrupt dealings, further tarnished his reputation. The perception that Rasputin was manipulating the royal family for his gain fueled widespread animosity and suspicion.

As World War I ravaged Europe and domestic discontent simmered in Russia, Rasputin's influence became a focal point of criticism. The war exacerbated the nation's economic and social woes, leading to growing unrest among the population. Many Russians blamed Rasputin for the country's misfortunes, believing his advice to the Tsar was detrimental to the war effort and governance. This sentiment was shared by members of the aristocracy and military who believed Rasputin's removal was essential for the survival of the Russian state.

The plot to assassinate Rasputin was orchestrated by a group of nobles, including Prince Felix Yusupov, Grand Duke Dmitri Pavlovich, and right-wing politician Vladimir Purishkevich. They believed that Rasputin's death would restore stability and remove the malign influence over the Tsar and Tsarina. On the night of December 29, 1916, the conspirators invited Rasputin to Yusupov's palace under the pretense of meeting Yusupov's wife, Princess Irina, a ruse designed to lure Rasputin to his death.

The details of Rasputin's assassination are shrouded in mystery and conflicting accounts, contributing to the enduring fascination with his death. According to Yusupov's memoirs, Rasputin was served cakes and wine laced with cyanide. Remarkably, the poison appeared to have little effect on him, which baffled the conspirators. Desperate to complete their mission, Yusupov retrieved a revolver and shot Rasputin in the chest. Believing him to be dead, the conspirators celebrated prematurely, only for Rasputin to stagger to his feet and attempt to flee.

In a panic, the conspirators shot Rasputin multiple times before clubbing him into submission. They then bound his body, wrapped it in a carpet, and threw it into the icy Neva River. When Rasputin's body was recovered a few days later, it was reportedly found with his hands free and in a position suggesting he had tried to untie his bonds, leading to the chilling belief that he had been alive when thrown into the river and had ultimately drowned.

The exact sequence of events and the accuracy of Yusupov's account have been subjects of debate and speculation. Some historians argue that the poisoning may have been fabricated or exaggerated, while others suggest that Rasputin's reputed resilience to the poison could be attributed to his habitual heavy drinking, which might have rendered him less susceptible to its effects. The discrepancies and sensational elements of Rasputin's assassination have spawned numerous myths and conspiracies, adding layers of intrigue to his already enigmatic persona.

Rasputin's death did little to stabilize the Russian monarchy or quell the rising tide of revolution. In fact, it may have hastened the downfall of the Romanovs. The February Revolution of 1917, a few months after Rasputin's assassination, led to the abdication of Tsar Nicholas II and the eventual execution of the royal family by Bolshevik revolutionaries. The elimination of Rasputin, once seen as a potential savior for the monarchy, became a symbol of the royal family's isolation from reality and their inability to address the nation's pressing issues.

Rasputin's legacy is multifaceted, encompassing his role as a mystic healer, a trusted advisor, and a scapegoat for the failures of the Romanov regime. His life and death have inspired countless books, films, and academic studies, each attempting to unravel the truth behind the myths and legends. Rasputin remains a figure of fascination, embodying the turbulence and complexity of early 20th-century Russia.

In the years following his death, Rasputin's influence on Russian history continued to be a subject of intense scrutiny. His alleged prophecies, including one that foretold his own death and the subsequent downfall of the Romanovs, have been cited as evidence of his supernatural abilities. Whether viewed as a saintly healer or a malevolent manipulator, Rasputin's impact on Russian history is undeniable.

The narrative of Rasputin's life and death serves as a cautionary tale about the dangers of unchecked influence and the susceptibility of power to manipulation. It also reflects the broader socio-political dynamics of pre-revolutionary Russia, where desperation and disillusionment created fertile ground for charismatic figures like Rasputin to emerge and thrive. His story, marked by drama, controversy, and mystery, continues to captivate and provoke debate, ensuring that Rasputin's enigmatic legacy endures well into the 21st century.

Chapter 14: The Unsolved Murder of JonBenét Ramsey

The unsolved murder of JonBenét Ramsey remains one of the most perplexing and infamous cases in American criminal history. JonBenét, a six-year-old child beauty pageant contestant, was found dead in her family's home in Boulder, Colorado, on December 26, 1996. The case has captivated the public's attention for decades, spawning numerous theories, books, documentaries, and media coverage. Despite extensive investigations, the identity of her killer remains unknown, making it one of the most enduring mysteries in modern times.

JonBenét Patricia Ramsey was born on August 6, 1990, to Patricia (Patsy) and John Ramsey. The family, including JonBenét's older brother Burke, lived a seemingly idyllic life. JonBenét participated in numerous beauty pageants, winning titles and drawing media attention due to her striking looks and poised performances. The Ramsey family appeared to be living the American dream, but the tragic events of December 1996 would shatter that image forever.

On the morning of December 26, 1996, Patsy Ramsey discovered a ransom note on the staircase of their home, demanding $118,000 for JonBenét's safe return. The note, which was unusually long and written on paper from the Ramseys' home, directed John Ramsey to withdraw the exact amount of his recent bonus and await further instructions. Despite the note's warning not to contact the police, Patsy immediately called 911 at 5:52 a.m. to report her daughter missing.

Police arrived at the scene and began their investigation. However, several critical mistakes were made in the early hours of the case. The home was not properly secured, and friends and family were allowed to come and go, potentially contaminating the crime scene. Officers also failed to conduct a thorough search of the entire house initially. It wasn't until around 1:00 p.m. that John Ramsey, accompanied by family friend Fleet White, discovered JonBenét's body in the basement. She had been strangled with a garrote fashioned from a paintbrush handle and cord, and her skull had been fractured by a blow to the head. A piece of duct tape was found over her mouth, and her wrists were loosely bound with cord.

The autopsy revealed that JonBenét had suffered a severe blow to the head, which caused a fracture of her skull. The official cause of death was asphyxia due to strangulation associated with craniocerebral trauma. There were also indications of vaginal injury, leading some investigators to speculate about the possibility of sexual assault. The evidence suggested that JonBenét had been killed sometime during the night of December 25-26.

The investigation into JonBenét's murder was marked by controversy and missteps from the outset. The Boulder Police Department's handling of the case was widely criticized for its lack of experience with homicide investigations and its failure to secure the crime scene. The initial focus of the investigation was heavily directed at the Ramsey family, particularly Patsy and John. The unusual nature of the ransom note, the fact that it was written on paper from the Ramseys' home, and the circumstances of the discovery of JonBenét's body all contributed to suspicions about the family's involvement.

The ransom note itself became a focal point of the investigation. Handwriting experts were brought in to analyze it, but the results were inconclusive. While Patsy Ramsey's handwriting bore some similarities to the note, it was not a definitive match. The peculiarities of the note, including its length, the specific amount of money demanded, and the use of phrases that seemed to mimic language from popular crime movies, added to the mystery.

In addition to the note, forensic evidence collected from the crime scene provided critical, yet puzzling, clues. A partial DNA profile was obtained from bloodstains found on JonBenét's underwear, which did not match any family members. However, this DNA did not match any known suspects in criminal databases at the time, leading to further questions about its origin. Other forensic evidence, including unidentified shoe prints and a palm print found in the basement, added to the complexity of the case.

As the investigation progressed, tensions between the Boulder Police Department and the Ramsey family escalated. The Ramseys hired high-profile defense attorneys and private investigators, further complicating the relationship with law enforcement. Public opinion was divided, with many believing that the Ramseys were involved in their daughter's death, while others felt they were being unfairly targeted.

The case took a significant turn in 1998 when the Boulder County District Attorney convened a grand jury to review the evidence. After 13 months of deliberation, the grand jury recommended charges of child abuse resulting in death against John and Patsy Ramsey. However, the District Attorney, Alex Hunter, declined to prosecute, citing insufficient evidence to prove guilt beyond a reasonable doubt. This decision only fueled public speculation and controversy surrounding the case.

In the years that followed, various theories emerged regarding JonBenét's murder. One prominent theory suggested that an intruder had entered the Ramsey home and killed JonBenét. Proponents of this theory pointed to the unknown DNA, the presence of an unidentified shoe print, and the possibility of a forced entry. Critics of the intruder theory argued that the absence of clear signs of a break-in and the use of items from the Ramsey home to commit the crime undermined this scenario.

Another theory posited that JonBenét's death was the result of an accidental injury, possibly inflicted by her brother Burke, and subsequently covered up by the parents. Advocates of this theory cited behavioral patterns and past incidents involving Burke, as well as inconsistencies in the Ramseys' statements. However, this theory, like others, lacked conclusive evidence and remained speculative.

In 2008, the case took another dramatic turn when new DNA testing techniques identified previously undetected genetic material on JonBenét's clothing. This new DNA evidence, which belonged to an unknown male, led the Boulder District Attorney, Mary Lacy, to publicly exonerate the Ramsey family, stating that they were no longer considered suspects. The announcement reignited public interest in the case and shifted the focus back to the possibility of an unknown intruder.

Despite the official exoneration, skepticism and debate continued. Some critics argued that the DNA evidence was not definitive proof of innocence and could have been the result of secondary transfer or contamination. Others maintained that the initial focus on the Ramsey family had hindered the investigation and that critical leads had been overlooked.

In the years since JonBenét's murder, numerous books, documentaries, and television specials have explored the case, each offering different perspectives and theories. High-profile figures in law enforcement, forensic science, and criminology have weighed in, adding their voices to the ongoing debate. The case remains a subject of intense public fascination and speculation, with new information and theories periodically emerging.

One of the enduring legacies of the JonBenét Ramsey case is its impact on how child murders and high-profile investigations are conducted. The mishandling of the initial investigation highlighted the need for better training and protocols for law enforcement in handling such sensitive cases. The media's role in shaping public perception and influencing the investigation also came under scrutiny, as the relentless coverage and sensationalism often obscured the search for truth.

The unsolved murder of JonBenét Ramsey continues to haunt those involved in the investigation and the public at large. The quest for justice for JonBenét remains unfulfilled, leaving a lingering sense of unresolved tragedy. Her death serves as a stark reminder of the complexities and challenges inherent in criminal investigations, particularly those involving young victims.

As of today, the case remains open, with law enforcement periodically reviewing new leads and advancements in forensic science offering hope that one day, the truth may be uncovered. The enduring mystery of JonBenét's murder ensures that her story will continue to be a subject of public interest and a poignant symbol of the quest for justice in the face of seemingly insurmountable odds.

Chapter 15: The Disappearance of Glenn Miller

The disappearance of Glenn Miller, the famed American big band leader, composer, and trombonist, is one of the enduring mysteries of the 20th century. Glenn Miller's contributions to music and his untimely disappearance during World War II have left an indelible mark on history. Born on March 1, 1904, in Clarinda, Iowa, Glenn Miller became a household name in the 1930s and 1940s with hits like "In the Mood," "Moonlight Serenade," and "Chattanooga Choo Choo." His band, the Glenn Miller Orchestra, was one of the most popular and influential musical groups of the swing era.

In the early 1940s, as World War II intensified, Miller felt a patriotic duty to contribute to the war effort. Despite his success in the civilian music industry, he enlisted in the U.S. Army in 1942. Miller was soon commissioned as a captain in the Army Air Forces and tasked with modernizing military band music to boost troop morale. He formed the Army Air Force Band, which performed extensively for troops in Europe, often under challenging conditions.

On December 15, 1944, Glenn Miller boarded a single-engine C-64 Norseman aircraft in England. He was en route to Paris to make arrangements for a performance to entertain Allied troops during the Battle of the Bulge. The weather was cold and foggy, typical for that time of year. The plane, piloted by Flight Officer John R. S. Morgan, took off from RAF Twinwood Farm airfield near Bedford. Also on board was Lieutenant Colonel Norman Baessell. Tragically, the aircraft never reached its destination, and Glenn Miller was never seen again.

The disappearance of Glenn Miller was met with shock and disbelief. Initial efforts to locate the missing plane were hampered by poor weather and the chaotic wartime environment. Despite extensive searches, no trace of the aircraft, Miller, or the other passengers was found. The official explanation was that the plane likely crashed into the English Channel due to bad weather or mechanical failure. However, the absence of concrete evidence has led to numerous theories and speculations over the years.

One popular theory suggests that the aircraft was accidentally struck by bombs jettisoned by returning RAF bombers. On the day of Miller's flight, several RAF bombers returning from an aborted mission over Germany were instructed to jettison their bomb loads over the English Channel before landing. Some researchers believe that Miller's plane could have been inadvertently caught in the path of these jettisoned bombs, leading to its destruction.

Another theory posits that Miller's plane experienced mechanical failure. The Norseman aircraft was known to have carburetor issues that could cause engine failure, particularly in cold weather. This theory suggests that icing on the carburetor might have caused the engine to fail, leading to a crash into the icy waters of the Channel. However, without wreckage or definitive evidence, this remains speculative.

Conspiracy theories have also emerged over the years. Some claim that Miller was on a secret mission for the Allies and was either captured or killed by enemy forces. Others suggest that he survived the crash and lived out his days under an assumed identity. These theories, while intriguing, lack credible evidence and are widely considered to be speculative at best.

The U.S. and British governments conducted investigations into Miller's disappearance. The U.S. Army Air Forces officially listed Miller as missing in action, and subsequent inquiries concluded that the most likely cause was a crash into the English Channel. However, the lack of physical evidence and the many unanswered questions have kept the mystery alive.

Over the decades, various expeditions and searches have been undertaken to locate the wreckage of Miller's plane. In 1987, a fisherman claimed to have found the remains of a Norseman aircraft off the coast of France, but subsequent searches failed to confirm the discovery. The search for definitive answers continues to this day, driven by both historical interest and the desire to bring closure to one of World War II's enduring enigmas.

Glenn Miller's legacy as a musician and bandleader is significant. His distinctive sound, characterized by a clarinet-led reed section, innovative arrangements, and smooth, melodic style, left an indelible mark on the swing era and popular music. His contributions to the war effort through his music and dedication to entertaining troops earned him a special place in American history.

Miller's disappearance has been the subject of numerous books, documentaries, and films, each exploring different aspects of his life, career, and mysterious fate. His story is a testament to the enduring power of music and the human spirit, as well as the uncertainties and tragedies of war.

Despite the passage of time, interest in Glenn Miller's disappearance remains strong. In 2019, new efforts were made to analyze historical records and eyewitness accounts in the hope of uncovering new leads. Advances in technology, such as improved sonar and underwater exploration equipment, offer renewed hope that the mystery might one day be solved. However, until definitive evidence is found, the disappearance of Glenn Miller will continue to intrigue and mystify.

The impact of Miller's disappearance extends beyond the realm of music and into the broader cultural and historical context of World War II. His dedication to boosting troop morale through music highlights the important role of arts and entertainment in maintaining the spirits of those involved in the war effort. Miller's story also underscores the risks faced by those who served, not only on the front lines but also in support roles, and the many untold stories of sacrifice and loss.

In reflecting on the life and legacy of Glenn Miller, one is reminded of the profound influence of his music, which continues to resonate with audiences today. His recordings remain popular, and his contributions to the development of big band music are celebrated by musicians and historians alike. The Glenn Miller Orchestra, reformed after his death, continues to perform and tour, keeping his music alive for new generations.

The mystery of Glenn Miller's disappearance serves as a poignant reminder of the many unresolved questions and unsolved mysteries from World War II. It is a story that combines elements of fame, tragedy, and intrigue, capturing the imagination and interest of people around the world. As we continue to seek answers, the legacy of Glenn Miller endures, a testament to his talent, dedication, and the enduring power of his music.

Chapter 16: The Mysterious Death of Natalie Wood

The mysterious death of Natalie Wood remains one of Hollywood's most enduring unsolved mysteries, steeped in speculation, controversy, and a legacy of unanswered questions. Natalie Wood, an acclaimed actress known for her roles in classic films such as "West Side Story," "Rebel Without a Cause," and "Splendor in the Grass," died under suspicious circumstances on November 29, 1981. She was only 43 years old. Her death was initially ruled an accidental drowning, but subsequent investigations and emerging evidence have kept the case alive in the public's imagination and the media spotlight for decades.

Natalie Wood was born Natalia Nikolaevna Zakharenko on July 20, 1938, in San Francisco, California, to Russian immigrant parents. She began her acting career at a young age, quickly becoming a child star with her role in "Miracle on 34th Street" at the age of eight. As she transitioned into adulthood, Wood successfully navigated the often treacherous path from child star to respected actress, earning three Academy Award nominations by the age of 25. Her beauty, talent, and charisma made her one of the most beloved figures in Hollywood.

The circumstances surrounding Wood's death began on the evening of November 28, 1981. She was on a weekend boat trip aboard the Splendour, a 55-foot yacht, off the coast of Santa Catalina Island in California. Accompanying her were her husband, actor Robert Wagner; her co-star from the film "Brainstorm," Christopher Walken; and the boat's captain, Dennis Davern. The four of them had spent the day drinking and socializing. According to accounts, an argument broke out between Wagner and Walken, reportedly about Wood's career and her relationship with Walken. Tensions escalated, and Wood eventually left the group to retire to her cabin.

The exact details of what happened next remain unclear. Sometime during the night, Wood went missing. Wagner and Davern searched the boat but could not find her. They eventually discovered that the dinghy, which had been tied to the yacht, was also missing. At around 1:30 a.m. on November 29, Wagner radioed the Coast Guard to report Wood missing. Her body was found floating in the water about a mile away from the yacht later that morning. She was dressed in a nightgown, socks, and a down jacket.

The initial investigation concluded that Wood had accidentally drowned. The coroner's report noted that she had a blood alcohol level of 0.14 percent, along with traces of a motion sickness medication and painkiller, which may have impaired her judgment. It was theorized that she had slipped while trying to board the dinghy, fallen into the water, and drowned. Bruises on her body were attributed to the fall, and no foul play was suspected at the time. However, this explanation did not satisfy everyone, and suspicions persisted.

In the years following her death, numerous inconsistencies and conflicting accounts began to emerge. Captain Dennis Davern, in particular, changed his story multiple times. Initially, he supported the accidental drowning narrative, but in later interviews and a 2009 book co-written with journalist Marti Rulli titled "Goodbye Natalie, Goodbye Splendour," he claimed that Wagner had been involved in Wood's death. Davern alleged that Wagner and Wood had a violent argument that night, and Wagner had instructed him not to turn on the searchlights or immediately notify authorities when Wood went missing.

Davern's new account reignited public interest and prompted authorities to reopen the case. In 2011, on the 30th anniversary of Wood's death, the Los Angeles County Sheriff's Department officially reopened the investigation, citing new information provided by Davern and others. This new inquiry brought renewed scrutiny to the events of that fateful night and raised questions about the thoroughness of the original investigation.

In 2012, the Los Angeles County coroner's office amended Wood's death certificate to change the cause of death from "accidental drowning" to "drowning and other undetermined factors." The report noted that the bruises on Wood's body might have occurred before she entered the water, suggesting that she may have been injured during an altercation. The coroner's office also criticized the original investigation for not thoroughly examining these injuries.

Despite the reopened investigation and the reclassification of Wood's death, definitive answers remained elusive. Robert Wagner, who had remarried and largely avoided public comment on the matter, became a person of interest in the case. In 2018, the Los Angeles County Sheriff's Department named Wagner as a person of interest, citing inconsistencies in his statements and the new testimony from Davern. However, no charges were filed, and Wagner has consistently denied any wrongdoing, maintaining that Wood's death was a tragic accident.

The mystery surrounding Natalie Wood's death has continued to captivate the public and inspire numerous books, documentaries, and media coverage. Theories about what happened range from accidental drowning due to intoxication and rough seas, to foul play involving Wagner or others on the boat. The involvement of high-profile Hollywood figures and the dramatic circumstances have fueled ongoing speculation and debate.

Wood's death also highlighted issues related to domestic violence, alcohol abuse, and the challenges of investigating cases involving celebrities. The case has often been compared to other high-profile Hollywood tragedies, where the intersection of fame, personal turmoil, and untimely death created a perfect storm of mystery and intrigue.

In addition to the legal and investigative aspects, the personal impact on those close to Wood cannot be overlooked. Her daughters,

Natasha Gregson Wagner and Courtney Wagner, have spoken about the profound loss and the toll the unresolved questions have taken on their lives. Natasha, in particular, has been vocal in defending her stepfather Robert Wagner and expressing skepticism about the theories of foul play. She has emphasized the need to remember her mother for her accomplishments and vibrant life, rather than just the tragic circumstances of her death.

The cultural and historical significance of Natalie Wood's life and career adds another layer to the mystery of her death. As an iconic figure of Hollywood's golden age, her performances and legacy continue to be celebrated. Her untimely death has also served as a cautionary tale about the pressures and pitfalls of fame, as well as the complexities of personal relationships in the public eye.

As of now, the case remains officially open, with authorities occasionally reviewing new information and leads. Advances in forensic technology and the persistence of those seeking answers offer some hope that one day, the full truth about what happened to Natalie Wood may be uncovered. Until then, the mystery endures, a haunting chapter in the annals of Hollywood history and a poignant reminder of the fragility of life, even for those who seem to have it all.

Chapter 17: The Enigma of the Zodiac Killer

The enigma of the Zodiac Killer is one of the most enduring and perplexing mysteries in American criminal history. Active primarily in the late 1960s and early 1970s, the Zodiac Killer is believed to be responsible for at least five confirmed murders in Northern California, although he claimed to have killed 37 people. The killer taunted police and the public with cryptic letters and ciphers, many of which have never been solved. Despite extensive investigations and numerous suspects, the Zodiac Killer was never caught, leaving behind a legacy of fear, speculation, and unanswered questions.

The Zodiac Killer's confirmed reign of terror began on December 20, 1968, with the murder of high school students Betty Lou Jensen and David Faraday on a secluded road near Vallejo, California. The couple had been on their first date and were parked in a lover's lane when they were attacked. Faraday was shot in the head at close range, while Jensen was shot multiple times as she attempted to flee. There were no witnesses, and the case initially baffled investigators.

The killer struck again on July 4, 1969, when Darlene Ferrin and Michael Mageau were shot while sitting in a parked car at a similar lover's lane location in Vallejo. Ferrin was killed, but Mageau survived despite being shot multiple times. Just an hour later, the Vallejo Police Department received a phone call from a man claiming responsibility for both the Ferrin-Mageau and the Jensen-Faraday murders. The caller provided details that had not been released to the public, establishing a clear link between the two incidents.

On August 1, 1969, the San Francisco Chronicle, San Francisco Examiner, and Vallejo Times-Herald received nearly identical letters from the Zodiac Killer. Each letter began with the phrase "Dear Editor: This is the Zodiac speaking" and included details of the murders that only the killer would know. The letters also contained a cryptogram consisting of 408 characters, which the killer claimed would reveal his identity. The Zodiac demanded that the letters be published on the front pages of the newspapers, threatening to kill again if they were not. The cryptogram, known as the "Zodiac 408," was solved by a couple from Salinas, California, who deciphered the message to read, "I like killing people because it is so much fun," among other chilling statements. However, the cipher did not reveal the killer's identity as promised.

The Zodiac struck again on September 27, 1969, when he attacked Bryan Hartnell and Cecelia Shepard at Lake Berryessa. The couple was picnicking by the lake when a man wearing an executioner's hood, sunglasses, and a bib-like garment with a cross-circle symbol approached them. He tied them up before brutally stabbing them both. Shepard succumbed to her injuries, but Hartnell survived and provided a detailed description of the attacker. After the attack, the Zodiac called the Napa County Sheriff's office from a payphone to report the crime, once again providing details only the killer would know.

On October 11, 1969, the Zodiac committed his last confirmed murder. Paul Stine, a San Francisco cab driver, was shot in the head at point-blank range in the city's Presidio Heights neighborhood. Unlike previous attacks, this crime occurred in an urban setting, and several witnesses saw the suspect leave the scene. Despite these sightings, the killer managed to evade capture. The Zodiac sent a letter to the San Francisco Chronicle three days later, mocking the police and including a piece of Stine's bloody shirt as proof of his involvement. This letter marked a turning point, as the Zodiac began to focus more on taunting the authorities and the media rather than committing further murders.

The Zodiac continued to send letters and ciphers to newspapers, with the final confirmed letter arriving in 1974. In these correspondences, he bragged about his supposed murders, criticized the police, and offered cryptic clues about his identity. The Zodiac's letters often included references to classic films, literature, and various cryptographic puzzles, suggesting he was well-read and enjoyed playing mind games with his pursuers. Despite the efforts of amateur and professional codebreakers, several of the Zodiac's ciphers remain unsolved, including the infamous "Zodiac 340" sent in November 1969.

Over the years, the Zodiac case has been the subject of numerous books, documentaries, and films. Various suspects have been proposed, but none have been definitively linked to the crimes. One of the most notable suspects was Arthur Leigh Allen, a convicted child molester with a history of violent behavior. Allen was identified by several people who claimed he had spoken about his desire to kill people and use the name "Zodiac" before the crimes were publicized. Despite these suspicions, there was no conclusive evidence linking Allen to the murders, and he died in 1992 without ever being charged.

Other suspects have included individuals ranging from a former newspaper cartoonist to a man with connections to the Manson Family. However, no one has ever been definitively proven to be the Zodiac Killer. The lack of physical evidence, combined with the killer's apparent ability to evade capture and his penchant for misleading clues, has made solving the case extraordinarily difficult. Advances in forensic technology, such as DNA profiling, have offered some hope, but thus far have not yielded a definitive suspect.

In 2020, a team of codebreakers announced they had solved the "Zodiac 340" cipher, which had baffled investigators for over 50 years. The solution revealed another taunting message but did not provide any new clues about the killer's identity. The message read, in part, "I hope you are having lots of fun in trying to catch me," underscoring the Zodiac's enjoyment of the cat-and-mouse game he played with law enforcement and the media.

The Zodiac's impact on popular culture and criminal investigations is significant. His case has inspired countless works of fiction, including novels, movies, and television series, often focusing on the themes of obsession, fear, and the elusiveness of justice. The Zodiac's ability to manipulate the media and public opinion through his letters and ciphers set a precedent for future serial killers who sought fame and notoriety through their crimes.

The case also highlighted the challenges faced by law enforcement in dealing with serial killers, particularly those who are highly intelligent and methodical. The Zodiac's ability to avoid capture despite leaving numerous clues and his continued taunting of the police demonstrated the difficulties in piecing together disparate pieces of evidence and coordinating efforts across different jurisdictions.

Despite the passage of time, interest in the Zodiac case remains high. Amateur sleuths and professional investigators continue to pore over the evidence, hoping to find the key that will unlock the mystery. Advances in technology, such as artificial intelligence and improved DNA analysis, offer new avenues for investigation, and there remains hope that one day the Zodiac Killer's identity will be revealed.

Chapter 18: The Disappearance of D. B. Cooper

The disappearance of D.B. Cooper is one of the most enduring mysteries in American history, captivating the imagination of the public and inspiring countless theories and investigations. The story began on November 24, 1971, the day before Thanksgiving, when a man using the alias Dan Cooper (later mistakenly referred to as D.B. Cooper) hijacked a Northwest Orient Airlines flight between Portland, Oregon, and Seattle, Washington. His subsequent escape with $200,000 in ransom money and his disappearance into the wilderness have become the stuff of legend.

On that fateful day, the man known as Dan Cooper boarded Flight 305, a Boeing 727, in Portland. He was described as a middle-aged man, dressed in a business suit and carrying a briefcase. After takeoff, he handed a note to a flight attendant, Florence Schaffner, who initially thought it was a lonely businessman's phone number and dropped it in her purse without reading it. Cooper then leaned towards her and whispered that she should read the note because he had a bomb. The note indicated that he had a bomb in his briefcase, and when Schaffner, understandably shaken, asked to see it, he opened the case to reveal a jumble of wires, red sticks, and a battery.

Cooper's demands were clear: $200,000 in $20 bills, four parachutes (two primary and two reserve), and a fuel truck standing by in Seattle to refuel the plane for his further demands. Schaffner relayed the message to the cockpit, and the captain, William Scott, contacted air traffic control, which in turn informed local and federal authorities. The FBI, working with Northwest Orient, quickly assembled the ransom money from several Seattle-area banks, ensuring each bill was microfilmed to facilitate tracing.

Upon arrival in Seattle, the passengers were unaware of the hijacking situation and were told there was a minor mechanical issue to keep them calm. Cooper allowed the 36 passengers to disembark in exchange for the money and parachutes, maintaining a calm and polite demeanor throughout the ordeal. He then instructed the flight crew to refuel the aircraft and outlined his plan: he wanted to fly to Mexico City at the minimum airspeed possible without stalling the aircraft, at an altitude of 10,000 feet. He also specified that the landing gear remain deployed, the wing flaps lowered to 15 degrees, and the cabin remain unpressurized.

Despite his meticulous instructions, the FBI and the airline's pilots discussed the best way to fulfill Cooper's demands while attempting to manage the risk. Two fighter jets from McChord Air Force Base were scrambled to follow the airliner. After refueling, Flight 305 took off at 7:40 PM with Cooper, the pilot, the copilot, a flight engineer, and one flight attendant on board. The flight path chosen took the aircraft south, with the intention to refuel again in Reno, Nevada, if needed.

Around 8:00 PM, somewhere over the rugged terrain of southwestern Washington, near the Lewis River, Cooper did the unthinkable: he jumped out of the rear stairway of the aircraft with the ransom money and one of the parachutes. The plane was in the air, and it was a dark, rainy night with strong winds, making conditions extremely hazardous. Cooper's disappearance into the night marked the beginning of one of the greatest manhunts in FBI history.

Upon landing in Reno, the authorities quickly boarded the aircraft and confirmed that Cooper was no longer on board. The investigation that followed was one of the most extensive and exhaustive manhunts ever conducted. FBI agents, local law enforcement, and military personnel scoured the area where they believed Cooper might have landed. Despite their efforts, no trace of Cooper was found, and the dense forest and rough terrain hampered the search. The search area was vast, covering parts of Washington and Oregon, and it was compounded by the lack of precise information about the exact drop zone.

Over the years, various pieces of evidence have surfaced, fueling speculation and debate. In 1980, an eight-year-old boy named Brian Ingram found a decaying package containing $5,800 in $20 bills along the Columbia River near Vancouver, Washington. The serial numbers matched those of the ransom money given to Cooper, leading investigators to conclude that it was indeed part of Cooper's loot. This discovery reignited interest in the case and prompted further searches of the area, but no additional evidence was found.

Several suspects have been proposed over the years, but none have been definitively linked to the crime. One of the most prominent suspects was Richard Floyd McCoy, who hijacked a plane in a similar manner in 1972 and was later killed in a shootout with the FBI. However, differences in physical appearance and modus operandi led many to dismiss McCoy as Cooper. Another suspect, Duane Weber, confessed to being Cooper on his deathbed in 1995, but investigators found no substantial evidence to support his claim.

In 2011, the FBI announced that they were closing the active investigation into the D.B. Cooper case, citing the lack of new credible leads. However, the case remains officially open, and the FBI continues to receive tips and investigate any potential new information. Despite the closure of the active investigation, the mystery of D.B. Cooper continues to captivate the public and inspire amateur sleuths, researchers, and conspiracy theorists.

One of the most intriguing aspects of the D.B. Cooper case is the question of whether he survived the jump. The conditions on the night of the hijacking were extremely harsh, with cold temperatures, high winds, and heavy rain. Cooper was not dressed for a jump from 10,000 feet, nor was he equipped with specialized gear that would have increased his chances of survival. The terrain where he is believed to have landed is dense, mountainous, and unforgiving. Many believe that

Cooper likely perished in the jump, and his remains were never found due to the difficult search conditions and passage of time.

Others speculate that Cooper survived the jump and managed to escape, possibly with the help of accomplices. Some theories suggest that Cooper was a skilled paratrooper or had military training, which would have given him the expertise needed to survive such a daring escape. The fact that no body or significant remains were ever found lends some credence to the theory that he might have survived. However, the lack of any concrete evidence or credible sightings of Cooper post-hijacking makes this theory difficult to prove.

The cultural impact of the D.B. Cooper case is significant. The mystery has been the subject of numerous books, documentaries, and even a feature film. The story has become a part of American folklore, with Cooper often depicted as a modern-day Robin Hood figure, a daring anti-hero who outsmarted the authorities and vanished into thin air. This romanticized view of Cooper contrasts sharply with the reality of his actions, which involved endangering the lives of innocent passengers and committing a serious federal crime.

The case has also had a lasting impact on aviation security. In the aftermath of the hijacking, several changes were implemented to prevent similar incidents. The most notable was the installation of "Cooper vanes," a mechanical device that prevents the rear stairway of a Boeing 727 from being lowered in flight. Additionally, stricter security measures and screening procedures were introduced at airports to prevent hijackings and ensure passenger safety.

Chapter 19: The Death of Kurt Cobain

Kurt Cobain, the enigmatic frontman of the iconic band Nirvana, remains one of the most compelling figures in rock music history, both for his profound influence on the genre and the mysterious circumstances surrounding his death. On April 8, 1994, Cobain's lifeless body was discovered in his Seattle home by an electrician, sparking a whirlwind of speculation, conspiracy theories, and media frenzy that continues to this day. Cobain's death was officially ruled a suicide, the result of a self-inflicted shotgun wound, compounded by a lethal dose of heroin. However, the details and inconsistencies surrounding his demise have led many to question this conclusion and explore alternative explanations.

Cobain's rise to fame was meteoric, driven by Nirvana's breakthrough album "Nevermind," which catapulted the band into the mainstream and established them as the leaders of the grunge movement. Despite his success, Cobain struggled with the pressures of fame, chronic health issues, and a long-standing battle with addiction. His tumultuous personal life, including his volatile relationship with wife Courtney Love, added to his emotional turmoil. Cobain's artistry was deeply intertwined with his pain and alienation, themes that resonated with a generation but also seemed to foreshadow his tragic end.

In the weeks leading up to his death, Cobain's behavior became increasingly erratic. He had just returned from a stint in rehab following an overdose in Rome that was reported as an accident but later suspected to be a suicide attempt. Friends and family noted his despondency and withdrawal, yet many were shocked by the finality of his actions. The discovery of Cobain's body was accompanied by a note addressed to his childhood imaginary friend "Boddah," in which he expressed his feelings of inadequacy and his belief that he could no longer enjoy music or fame.

Despite the official ruling of suicide, several inconsistencies have fueled alternative theories. Critics of the suicide verdict point to the high levels of heroin found in Cobain's system, arguing that he would have been incapacitated, if not already dead, before he could have pulled the trigger. Additionally, the presence of a second set of fingerprints on the shotgun, the lack of a definitive timeline of events leading to his death, and the peculiarities in his suicide note have been cited as reasons to doubt the official narrative. Some theorists have even suggested foul play, with Courtney Love often being implicated, though no concrete evidence has ever substantiated these claims.

The media's portrayal of Cobain's death played a significant role in shaping public perception. Sensationalist headlines and invasive coverage often overshadowed the more nuanced aspects of his life and struggles. This media blitz contributed to the mythologizing of Cobain, painting him as the quintessential tortured artist, a narrative that, while compelling, may oversimplify the complexity of his experiences and the reality of his mental health issues.

Cobain's death also had a profound impact on the music world and his fanbase. He became a symbol of the darker side of fame, a cautionary tale about the pressures of the music industry, and an enduring icon of rebellion and authenticity. His influence is still felt in contemporary music, with countless artists citing him as an inspiration. The enduring mystery of his death has also ensured that he remains a subject of fascination and speculation, with documentaries, books, and investigative pieces continuing to explore the myriad facets of his life and demise.

In examining Cobain's death, it is crucial to consider the broader context of his mental health and the societal attitudes towards mental illness at the time. The early 1990s were not particularly enlightened when it came to understanding and supporting mental health issues, particularly in the high-stakes environment of the entertainment industry. Cobain's struggles with depression, chronic pain from an undiagnosed stomach condition, and addiction were well-documented, yet the resources and support available to him were limited. This lack of support undoubtedly played a role in the tragic outcome.

Moreover, Cobain's legacy is a reminder of the human cost of celebrity and the often-overlooked challenges that accompany fame. The music industry, with its relentless demands and invasive scrutiny, can be an unforgiving environment for those already grappling with personal demons. Cobain's life and death underscore the importance of mental health awareness and the need for comprehensive support systems for artists and public figures.

The death of Kurt Cobain remains a complex and multifaceted enigma, encompassing elements of personal struggle, societal pressures, and enduring mystery. While the official narrative points to suicide, the numerous inconsistencies and unanswered questions leave room for continued speculation and investigation. Cobain's influence on music and culture is indisputable, and his tragic end serves as a poignant reminder of the fragility of life and the profound impact of mental health. As fans and scholars continue to delve into the details of his death, Kurt Cobain's legacy lives on, not just through his music, but through the ongoing quest to understand the man behind the myth.

Chapter 20: The Mystery of the Dyatlov Pass Incident

The Dyatlov Pass Incident remains one of the most perplexing and haunting mysteries in modern history, capturing the imagination of researchers, conspiracy theorists, and the general public alike. This enigmatic event occurred in the winter of 1959 in the northern Ural Mountains of the Soviet Union, where a group of nine experienced hikers met a gruesome and inexplicable end. Despite extensive investigations and numerous theories, the true cause of their deaths remains shrouded in mystery, fostering a myriad of speculations that range from the plausible to the fantastical.

The group, led by 23-year-old Igor Dyatlov, was composed of eight men and two women, all of whom were students or graduates of the Ural Polytechnical Institute. They embarked on their journey in late January, aiming to reach Otorten, a mountain whose name ominously translates to "Don't go there" in the Mansi language. Initially, everything seemed to be proceeding according to plan. The group was well-prepared and equipped, and they maintained detailed diaries and took numerous photographs, providing a clear account of their journey up to a certain point.

On February 1, the hikers set up camp on the slopes of Kholat Syakhl, meaning "Dead Mountain" in the Mansi language. For reasons that remain unclear, they abandoned their campsite in the middle of the night, fleeing into the freezing wilderness inadequately dressed for the harsh conditions. The subsequent search operation, initiated when the group failed to return as scheduled, uncovered their bodies over the course of several months in various states of distress and disarray, scattered up to a mile away from their tent.

The initial discovery of the tent raised immediate questions. It had been slashed open from the inside, suggesting the hikers had left in a state of urgent panic. The first two bodies, those of Yuri Krivonischenko and Yuri Doroshenko, were found near the remains of a fire under a large cedar tree, clad only in their underwear. Nearby branches were broken up to five meters high, indicating someone had climbed the tree, possibly to look for something or someone. The next bodies discovered, including Dyatlov's, were found at varying distances, leading back towards the tent, as if they had attempted to return.

The most disturbing discoveries were the last four bodies, found buried under four meters of snow in a ravine, roughly 75 meters from the cedar tree. These individuals had suffered severe injuries: Ludmila Dubinina and Semyon Zolotaryov had major chest fractures, Nikolai Thibeaux-Brignolles had a significant skull fracture, and Dubinina was found missing her tongue, eyes, and part of her lips. Despite the trauma, there were no external wounds corresponding to the internal damage, and forensic experts compared the force required to inflict such injuries to that of a car crash. Additionally, some of the hikers' clothing was found to be radioactive, adding another layer of mystery to the already baffling incident.

The official investigation, concluded in May 1959, was inconclusive, stating that the hikers had died due to "a compelling natural force." The case was promptly closed, and the files were archived, leading to widespread speculation and the development of numerous theories over the subsequent decades. The lack of clear answers and the unusual details of the case fostered a fertile ground for speculation, and various explanations have been proposed, ranging from the plausible to the outlandish.

One of the earliest theories suggested an avalanche might have forced the hikers to flee their tent in panic. However, this theory is largely dismissed by experts, as the terrain did not show typical signs of an avalanche, and the injuries sustained by the hikers were not consistent with such an event. Another theory posits that katabatic winds, which are powerful and descending winds capable of creating a sudden and extreme drop in temperature, might have played a role. These winds could have produced an infrasound phenomenon, causing panic and disorientation among the hikers, leading them to irrationally abandon their tent.

Other theories venture into the realm of the supernatural or extraterrestrial. Some speculate that the hikers might have encountered a yeti or some other unknown creature, driven them out of their tent in terror. Another popular hypothesis involves UFOs, suggesting that the hikers might have witnessed an extraterrestrial event, leading to their frantic escape and subsequent deaths. These theories, while intriguing, lack substantial evidence and are generally considered speculative at best.

Military involvement is another frequently discussed angle. Some propose that the hikers inadvertently stumbled upon secret military tests, such as parachute mines or rocket launches, which could explain the strange injuries and the radioactive clothing. The Soviet Union's secrecy during the Cold War era adds a layer of plausibility to this theory, as does the presence of unusual metal fragments and reports of glowing orbs in the sky by other witnesses in the area around the same time.

Further complicating the mystery are reports of possible espionage. Some researchers suggest that at least two members of the group might have been KGB agents on a mission to rendezvous with foreign agents or intercept sensitive information. This theory posits that the hikers' deaths were the result of a covert operation gone wrong, either through exposure to experimental weaponry or direct conflict. While intriguing, this theory also relies heavily on circumstantial evidence and speculation.

In recent years, renewed interest in the Dyatlov Pass Incident has led to further investigations and technological analyses. A 2019 study utilized computer simulations and forensic recreations, supporting the possibility of a small-scale avalanche, also known as a "slab avalanche," which might have caused the initial panic without leaving typical signs. This hypothesis aligns with some of the physical evidence but still fails to account for all the peculiarities, such as the radiation and the severe internal injuries.

The cultural impact of the Dyatlov Pass Incident cannot be overstated. It has inspired numerous books, documentaries, and films, each attempting to piece together the fragmented and enigmatic narrative. The incident taps into deep-seated fears of the unknown, blending elements of survival horror, conspiracy, and the supernatural. It serves as a potent reminder of nature's unforgiving power and the limits of human understanding in the face of unexplained phenomena.

Ultimately, the Dyatlov Pass Incident remains an enduring mystery, a puzzle with pieces that refuse to fit neatly together. It challenges our perceptions of what we can know and understand about the world and our place in it. The unanswered questions continue to haunt the memories of the nine hikers and fuel the search for truth, keeping the story alive in the annals of unsolved mysteries. As new theories and technologies emerge, there is always the hope that one day, the full story of what happened on that fateful night in 1959 will finally be revealed, bringing closure to one of the most haunting enigmas of the 20th century.

Chapter 21: The Unsolved Death of Elisa Lam

The mysterious death of Elisa Lam has intrigued and puzzled people around the world, becoming a modern urban legend with unsettling and baffling details. Elisa Lam, a 21-year-old Canadian student from the University of British Columbia, was found dead in the water tank of the Cecil Hotel in Los Angeles on February 19, 2013. Her death was officially ruled as an accidental drowning, but the circumstances surrounding her disappearance and the discovery of her body have sparked numerous theories and widespread speculation.

Elisa Lam traveled to Los Angeles alone as part of a solo trip along the West Coast. She checked into the Cecil Hotel on January 26, 2013. The Cecil Hotel itself has a dark and storied history, having been the site of numerous suicides, murders, and housing infamous criminals such as serial killers Richard Ramirez and Jack Unterweger. This reputation added an eerie backdrop to the events that would unfold.

Lam was initially assigned a shared room, but after her roommates complained about her odd behavior, she was moved to a room by herself. Her behavior in the days leading up to her disappearance was documented through her blog posts and social media updates, which painted a picture of a young woman struggling with mental health issues, including bipolar disorder and depression. These entries provided insight into her state of mind, but they also raised questions about what exactly led to her untimely death.

The last known sighting of Elisa Lam was on January 31, 2013, captured by a surveillance camera in one of the hotel's elevators. This footage became infamous after it was released to the public by the LAPD in a bid to gather information on her whereabouts. In the video, Lam is seen behaving erratically. She enters the elevator and presses multiple buttons, peering out of the elevator as if hiding from someone or something. At times, she steps out of the elevator, gestures strangely, and appears to be talking to someone unseen. Her odd behavior and the malfunctioning elevator, which remains open despite her pressing numerous buttons, have fueled countless theories about what happened to her.

Following her disappearance, a thorough search of the hotel and its premises was conducted by the LAPD, but no trace of Lam was found initially. It wasn't until February 19, 2013, when guests at the hotel began complaining about low water pressure and odd-tasting water, that maintenance workers investigated the water tanks on the roof of the hotel. To their shock, they discovered Lam's decomposing body inside one of the tanks. Her death was officially ruled an accidental drowning, with the coroner's report noting that she had a history of bipolar disorder, which might have contributed to her actions. The toxicology report showed traces of her prescribed medications, but no recreational drugs or alcohol were found in her system.

Despite the official ruling, several aspects of the case remain deeply puzzling. The first major question is how Lam accessed the water tank. The roof of the Cecil Hotel was secured with an alarm system, and access was restricted. Even if Lam managed to reach the roof, the water tanks themselves were large and covered with heavy lids, making it difficult to believe she could have climbed in on her own. Additionally, the fact that the alarm was not triggered suggests either a failure in the security system or some unknown way Lam could have bypassed it.

Another disturbing element is the elevator video. The footage, which has been viewed and analyzed extensively, leaves many questions unanswered. Some believe it shows Lam experiencing a psychotic episode, possibly due to her bipolar disorder. Others speculate that she might have been under the influence of an unknown substance, although the toxicology report did not support this theory. There are also those who suggest the possibility of foul play, arguing that Lam's behavior indicates she might have been hiding from someone who ultimately caused her death.

The timing and editing of the elevator video have also come under scrutiny. Viewers have pointed out apparent skips and anomalies in the footage, suggesting that portions may have been edited or removed. This has led to further speculation about a potential cover-up, either by the hotel or by someone else with access to the surveillance system. The eerie and inexplicable nature of the video has only added to the aura of mystery surrounding the case.

Several theories have emerged attempting to explain Lam's death. One of the most prominent is that she experienced a manic episode due to her bipolar disorder, which led her to act irrationally and ultimately resulted in her accidental drowning. Supporters of this theory point to her history of mental health issues and the medications found in her system. However, this does not fully explain how she managed to access the roof and the water tank without triggering any alarms or why her behavior in the elevator video appears so deliberate and unusual.

Another theory involves the paranormal. The Cecil Hotel's dark history and the strange circumstances of Lam's death have led some to speculate about supernatural involvement. Stories of hauntings and ghostly encounters at the hotel have been long-standing, and Lam's inexplicable behavior in the elevator video has been interpreted by some as evidence of otherworldly influences. While intriguing, there is no concrete evidence to support this theory.

There are also theories suggesting foul play. Some believe that Lam might have encountered someone with malicious intent, possibly a hotel employee or a guest, who either coerced or forced her onto the roof and into the water tank. The presence of unidentified fingerprints on the tank's lid and the lack of an alarm trigger could support this idea. However, no concrete suspects or evidence have ever been identified, leaving this theory speculative.

The case of Elisa Lam has had a significant cultural impact, inspiring numerous documentaries, podcasts, and internet sleuths who continue to analyze and debate the details of her death. Her story has become emblematic of the modern urban legend, blending elements of psychological thriller, true crime, and the supernatural. It serves as a stark reminder of the vulnerabilities of individuals with mental health issues and the potential dangers lurking in seemingly safe environments.

In examining Lam's death, it is essential to consider the broader context of mental health awareness and support. Her case highlights the importance of understanding and adequately addressing mental health issues, especially in young adults. It also underscores the need for better safety measures in public accommodations, such as hotels, to prevent similar tragedies from occurring.

The mystery of Elisa Lam's death remains unresolved, with many questions still unanswered. The confluence of bizarre circumstances, eerie video footage, and the dark history of the Cecil Hotel create a narrative that is both captivating and unsettling. As long as these questions persist, the story of Elisa Lam will continue to fascinate and haunt those who seek to uncover the truth behind her untimely and mysterious demise.

Chapter 22: The Mysterious Demise of Michael Jackson

Michael Jackson, the "King of Pop," remains one of the most influential and enigmatic figures in the history of music and entertainment. His life, filled with extraordinary talent, global fame, and personal struggles, ended abruptly and mysteriously on June 25, 2009, at the age of 50. Jackson's death was officially attributed to acute propofol and benzodiazepine intoxication, with the coroner ruling it a homicide. The circumstances surrounding his death, however, have led to widespread speculation, numerous conspiracy theories, and ongoing legal battles, creating a lasting intrigue around the final chapter of his life.

Born on August 29, 1958, Michael Joseph Jackson rose to fame as the youngest member of the Jackson 5, a Motown group formed with his siblings. His incredible talent and charisma quickly set him apart, leading to a successful solo career that redefined the music industry. Jackson's innovative music, groundbreaking videos, and iconic dance moves, including the legendary moonwalk, earned him an unparalleled level of fame. Albums like "Thriller," "Bad," and "Dangerous" broke sales records and garnered countless awards, solidifying his status as a global superstar.

Despite his professional success, Jackson's life was marred by personal challenges and controversies. His childhood, marked by rigorous rehearsals and an often abusive relationship with his father, Joe Jackson, left lasting scars. As an adult, Jackson faced intense media scrutiny, particularly regarding his changing appearance, eccentric behavior, and allegations of child sexual abuse. These allegations, first surfacing in the early 1990s and again in the early 2000s, severely damaged his reputation, although he was acquitted of all charges in a high-profile trial in 2005.

By the late 2000s, Jackson's health and financial situation were deteriorating. He faced mounting debt, and reports suggested he was struggling with various physical and mental health issues, including chronic pain, insomnia, and anxiety. In an effort to stage a comeback, Jackson announced the "This Is It" concert series in March 2009, a planned 50-show residency at London's O2 Arena. The concerts, set to begin in July 2009, were highly anticipated and sold out within hours, promising to revive Jackson's career and financial standing.

Preparations for the "This Is It" tour were intense, with Jackson undergoing grueling rehearsals and reportedly experiencing significant stress. To manage his insomnia and anxiety, he relied on a cocktail of prescription medications. Among these was propofol, a powerful anesthetic typically used in surgical settings, administered by his personal physician, Dr. Conrad Murray. On the morning of June 25, 2009, Jackson was found unresponsive in his bedroom at his rented mansion in Holmby Hills, Los Angeles. Efforts to revive him were unsuccessful, and he was pronounced dead at the Ronald Reagan UCLA Medical Center.

The immediate aftermath of Jackson's death was chaotic, with fans and media converging on the hospital and his home. The news of his passing dominated global headlines, overshadowing all other events. An outpouring of grief and tributes from fans, celebrities, and world leaders underscored his immense impact on popular culture. At the same time, questions about the circumstances of his death began to emerge, leading to an intensive investigation by law enforcement and the coroner's office.

The autopsy revealed that Jackson had died of acute propofol intoxication, with additional sedatives, including lorazepam and midazolam, contributing to the fatal overdose. Propofol, often referred to as "milk of amnesia" due to its milky appearance, is a powerful anesthetic used to induce and maintain sedation in surgical patients. Its use outside of a hospital setting, particularly for insomnia, is highly irregular and dangerous. The investigation focused on Dr. Conrad Murray, who had been hired by Jackson to manage his medical care during the tour preparations.

Murray admitted to administering propofol to Jackson on the night of his death, but he claimed that he did so at Jackson's insistence and that he had been trying to wean him off the drug. The investigation revealed that Murray had been negligent in his medical practice, failing to properly monitor Jackson after administering the drug and delaying the call for emergency assistance. Furthermore, Murray lacked the necessary equipment and expertise to safely administer propofol in a home setting.

In 2011, Dr. Conrad Murray was tried and convicted of involuntary manslaughter. He was sentenced to four years in prison but was released in 2013 after serving two years. The trial shed light on the extent of Jackson's drug use and the questionable practices of the medical professionals surrounding him. It also raised broader issues about the pressures of fame, the responsibilities of those entrusted with the care of high-profile individuals, and the dangers of prescription drug abuse.

Despite the official findings, various conspiracy theories about Jackson's death have persisted. Some fans and observers believe that foul play was involved, suggesting that Jackson was murdered as part of a larger plot. These theories often point to his significant debts, valuable music catalog, and ongoing legal battles as potential motives for those who might benefit from his death. Others speculate that Jackson faked his death to escape the relentless scrutiny and pressures of his life, citing alleged sightings and supposed inconsistencies in the official accounts as evidence.

Jackson's family, particularly his mother Katherine and siblings, have also voiced concerns about the circumstances of his death. They have questioned the role of AEG Live, the promoter of the "This Is It" concerts, and their handling of Jackson's health and well-being. The family filed a wrongful death lawsuit against AEG Live, alleging that the company had negligently hired and supervised Dr. Murray. The case went to trial in 2013, but the jury ultimately found that AEG Live was not liable for Jackson's death.

The mysterious demise of Michael Jackson continues to resonate, reflecting the complex and often tragic life of a man who was both a brilliant artist and a deeply troubled individual. His death highlighted the darker side of fame and the entertainment industry, where immense pressure and expectations can lead to destructive behaviors and choices. It also underscored the dangers of prescription drug abuse and the critical importance of responsible medical care.

Jackson's legacy is multifaceted, encompassing his extraordinary contributions to music, dance, and popular culture, as well as the controversies and scandals that plagued his personal life. His influence on subsequent generations of artists is undeniable, with his innovative work in music videos, stage performances, and philanthropy setting new standards and inspiring countless performers.

In the years since his death, Jackson's music and artistic achievements have continued to be celebrated, while his life story remains a subject of fascination and debate. Posthumous releases, documentaries, and tributes have sought to honor his legacy, while also grappling with the complexities and contradictions that defined him. The estate's ongoing efforts to manage and preserve his brand have resulted in substantial financial success, ensuring that Jackson's influence endures.

The mysterious demise of Michael Jackson serves as a poignant reminder of the human vulnerabilities behind the facade of celebrity. It challenges us to consider the costs of fame, the responsibilities of those in positions of care and trust, and the need for greater awareness and action regarding mental health and substance abuse. As the world continues to remember and celebrate Michael Jackson's unparalleled contributions to entertainment, the quest for a deeper understanding of his life and death remains a compelling and enduring pursuit.

Chapter 23: The Death of Vincent van Gogh

The death of Vincent van Gogh is one of the most enduring mysteries in the world of art, marked by controversy, speculation, and conflicting accounts. The Dutch post-impressionist painter, whose work profoundly influenced 20th-century art, died on July 29, 1890, at the age of 37, in the small village of Auvers-sur-Oise, France. Officially, his death was ruled a suicide due to a gunshot wound to the chest, but the circumstances surrounding his final days and the nature of his death have been the subject of intense debate.

Vincent van Gogh was born on March 30, 1853, in Groot-Zundert, Netherlands. His early life was marked by instability and a series of unsuccessful attempts at various careers, including working as an art dealer, teacher, and preacher. It was not until his late twenties that he decided to pursue a career as an artist. Despite receiving little formal training, van Gogh produced more than 2,100 artworks, including about 860 oil paintings, many of which were created during the last two years of his life.

Van Gogh's life was plagued by mental illness, poverty, and social isolation. He suffered from severe bouts of depression and psychotic episodes, which led to his infamous ear-cutting incident in 1888. This episode occurred while he was living in Arles, France, and resulted in his hospitalization. His mental health issues were compounded by a lack of financial stability and frequent conflicts with friends and colleagues, including fellow artist Paul Gauguin.

By May 1890, van Gogh moved to Auvers-sur-Oise to be closer to his brother Theo, who was his primary financial and emotional support. In Auvers, van Gogh was under the care of Dr. Paul Gachet, a homeopathic physician and amateur artist who had a reputation for treating mental illness. During this time, van Gogh was highly productive, creating more than 70 paintings in the last 70 days of his life, including some of his most famous works such as "Wheatfield with Crows" and "Portrait of Dr. Gachet."

On July 27, 1890, van Gogh sustained a gunshot wound to the chest. He managed to walk back to the Ravoux Inn, where he was staying. The local physician, Dr. Mazery, and Dr. Gachet were called to treat him, but the bullet was not removed, and he succumbed to his injuries two days later. His brother Theo, who arrived shortly after the shooting, was with him when he died. Van Gogh's reported last words were, "La tristesse durera toujours," or "The sadness will last forever."

The traditional narrative is that van Gogh shot himself in a wheat field, driven by despair and the belief that he was a burden to his brother Theo. This account is largely based on Theo's letters and the reports of those who were present in his final days. However, there are several inconsistencies and unanswered questions that have led to alternative theories about his death.

One of the main points of contention is the location and circumstances of the shooting. Van Gogh allegedly shot himself in the chest, a highly unusual method for suicide, especially considering the difficulties in positioning the gun and the likelihood of surviving such a wound long enough to return to the inn. Additionally, the gun was never found, and there were no witnesses to the shooting.

In 2011, authors Steven Naifeh and Gregory White Smith published a biography, "Van Gogh: The Life," which proposed an alternative theory that van Gogh might have been accidentally shot by two local boys, René and Gaston Secrétan. According to their research, the Secrétan brothers were known to have harassed van Gogh, and René had a penchant for playing with firearms. Naifeh and Smith suggest that van Gogh might have covered up the incident to protect the boys, thus explaining the lack of a suicide note and the discrepancies in the details of his death.

This theory is supported by some circumstantial evidence and the peculiar nature of van Gogh's wounds. The angle and location of the gunshot, as described in medical reports, suggest that it could have been fired from a distance rather than being self-inflicted. Additionally, van Gogh's calm demeanor and reluctance to explain the incident in detail could be interpreted as an attempt to shield the boys from blame.

Despite these arguments, the majority of art historians and scholars continue to support the suicide theory. Van Gogh's letters reveal a man who was deeply troubled and often spoke of his desire for peace and an end to his suffering. In the weeks leading up to his death, he wrote about feeling increasingly despondent and burdened by his illness and financial woes. His relationship with Dr. Gachet, which initially seemed promising, had also begun to deteriorate, adding to his sense of hopelessness.

Theo's letters to his wife, Jo, provide further insight into van Gogh's state of mind. In one letter, written shortly after Vincent's death, Theo described his brother's final moments and expressed his belief that Vincent had taken his own life out of desperation. Theo's account has been a crucial piece of evidence in supporting the suicide theory, as it reflects the immediate reaction and understanding of someone who was intimately familiar with Vincent's struggles.

The debate over van Gogh's death is further complicated by the broader context of his life and work. Van Gogh's art was a reflection of his inner turmoil and his relentless pursuit of meaning and beauty. His intense, emotional style and use of vibrant colors were groundbreaking, yet his work received little recognition during his lifetime. He sold only a few paintings and lived in poverty, relying heavily on Theo's financial support.

The posthumous recognition of van Gogh's genius has cast a long shadow over the circumstances of his death. His tragic end has become part of the mythology surrounding his life, contributing to the romanticized image of the tortured artist. This narrative has been perpetuated by popular culture, including Irving Stone's biographical novel "Lust for Life" and its subsequent film adaptation, which depicted van Gogh's life and struggles in vivid detail.

In the years since van Gogh's death, his work has achieved immense popularity and critical acclaim. His paintings, characterized by their bold, expressive brushwork and emotional intensity, have had a profound impact on modern art. Major exhibitions of his work draw huge crowds, and his paintings fetch record prices at auction. The legacy of his artistic genius is undeniable, yet the mystery of his death continues to fascinate and elude definitive explanation.

The death of Vincent van Gogh remains an enduring enigma, embodying the complexities of his life and the broader themes of suffering and creativity. Whether he died by his own hand or as the result of an accidental shooting, the tragedy of his premature death has only added to the mystique of his legacy. The unanswered questions and conflicting theories serve as a reminder of the elusiveness of historical truth and the ways in which our understanding of the past is shaped by interpretation and perspective.

As we continue to celebrate and study van Gogh's work, it is essential to approach his life and death with empathy and nuance. His story is not just one of artistic brilliance but also of profound human struggle. By examining the various facets of his life and the circumstances of his death, we gain a deeper appreciation for the man behind the masterpieces and the enduring impact of his vision.

Chapter 24: The Disappearance of Ambrose Bierce

The unexplained disappearance of Ambrose Bierce remains one of the most intriguing mysteries in American literary history. Ambrose Gwinnett Bierce, born on June 24, 1842, in Meigs County, Ohio, was a prolific writer, journalist, and satirist known for his sharp wit and cynical style. His works, including the short story "An Occurrence at Owl Creek Bridge" and the satirical dictionary "The Devil's Dictionary," cemented his reputation as a master of dark humor and a keen observer of the human condition. Despite his literary accomplishments, Bierce's life was marked by tragedy, controversy, and ultimately, an enigmatic disappearance that has baffled historians and scholars for over a century.

Bierce's early life was shaped by hardship and adventure. He was the tenth of thirteen children in a poor family and grew up in the harsh environment of rural Indiana. At the age of 19, he enlisted in the Union Army during the American Civil War, serving with distinction in several major battles, including Shiloh, Chickamauga, and the Siege of Corinth. His wartime experiences profoundly influenced his writing, imbuing it with a stark realism and a deep skepticism about human nature and the futility of war. After the war, Bierce settled in San Francisco, where he began his career as a journalist and writer, contributing to various newspapers and magazines.

Throughout his career, Bierce developed a reputation for his biting criticism and fearless journalism. He became known as "Bitter Bierce" for his acerbic wit and his uncompromising stance on corruption and hypocrisy. His columns often targeted politicians, businessmen, and other public figures, earning him both admiration and enmity. Despite his success, Bierce's personal life was fraught with difficulties. His marriage to Mary Ellen "Mollie" Day ended in separation, and he endured the loss of two of his three children, which only deepened his cynicism and sense of existential despair.

By the early 1900s, Bierce was in his seventies and facing declining health. He decided to embark on a journey to Mexico, which was then in the throes of a revolutionary upheaval led by figures such as Francisco Madero, Emiliano Zapata, and Pancho Villa. Bierce's motives for this journey remain unclear, but it is speculated that he was seeking adventure, a final escapade, or perhaps a meaningful end to his life. His fascination with death and the macabre, evident in his writings, may have also played a role in his decision to travel to a war-torn country.

Bierce's last known communication was a letter dated December 26, 1913, sent from the town of Chihuahua in northern Mexico. In the letter, addressed to his close friend and secretary, Carrie Christiansen, Bierce wrote cryptically, "As to me, I leave here tomorrow for an unknown destination." This message has since fueled endless speculation about his fate. After this letter, Bierce vanished without a trace, and despite numerous investigations and searches, no conclusive evidence of his whereabouts or final resting place has ever been found.

Several theories have emerged over the years to explain Bierce's disappearance. One of the most popular theories is that he joined Pancho Villa's revolutionary army. This idea is supported by Bierce's fascination with military life and his admiration for Villa, whom he considered a Robin Hood-like figure fighting for social justice. Some accounts suggest that Bierce may have been killed in battle or executed by Villa's forces, either intentionally or accidentally. However, no definitive records or eyewitness accounts have surfaced to confirm this theory.

Another theory posits that Bierce, weary of life and disillusioned by his personal and professional struggles, chose to end his own life in a remote location. His writings often explored themes of existential angst, and he had expressed suicidal thoughts in his correspondence. This theory is consistent with his final letter, which hinted at a deliberate departure to an "unknown destination." However, the absence of a body or any concrete evidence leaves this hypothesis in the realm of speculation.

A more outlandish theory suggests that Bierce was abducted or killed by bandits or rival factions within the Mexican Revolution. The chaotic and violent nature of the period makes this scenario plausible, as many foreigners who ventured into the conflict zones were kidnapped, robbed, or murdered. Yet, again, there is no verifiable evidence to support this claim, and it remains one of many possibilities in the absence of concrete facts.

The lack of definitive information about Bierce's fate has led to numerous myths and legends. Some accounts suggest he faked his own death to escape debts or personal issues and lived out his remaining years under an assumed identity. Others speculate that he became a recluse in a remote village or was taken in by sympathetic locals who kept his secret. These stories, though intriguing, are based largely on conjecture and hearsay, contributing to the enduring mystery rather than providing any real answers.

Bierce's disappearance has also inspired a wealth of literary and artistic interpretations. His enigmatic end, combined with his dark, often morbid writing style, has made him a subject of fascination for novelists, playwrights, and filmmakers. Works such as Carlos Fuentes' novel "The Old Gringo" and Robert A. Heinlein's science fiction story "Lost Legacy" explore fictionalized versions of Bierce's fate, blending historical fact with imaginative speculation. These cultural depictions have helped keep Bierce's story alive in the public imagination, ensuring that his legacy endures even as the details of his final days remain shrouded in mystery.

The unresolved nature of Bierce's disappearance also reflects broader themes in his work, particularly his preoccupation with the unknowable and the irrational aspects of human existence. Bierce's stories often explore the thin line between reality and illusion, sanity and madness, life and death. His own vanishing act can be seen as a fitting, albeit tragic, conclusion to a life spent probing the darkest corners of the human psyche.

The mystery of Ambrose Bierce's disappearance continues to captivate scholars and enthusiasts, prompting ongoing research and debate. New theories and potential leads occasionally emerge, but none have yet provided a definitive answer. The enigma of his fate remains one of the great unsolved cases in literary history, a testament to the enduring allure of mystery and the complexities of the human condition.

As we reflect on Bierce's life and work, it is important to acknowledge both his contributions to American literature and the profound personal struggles he endured. His legacy as a writer of dark humor and incisive social commentary is secure, but the unresolved questions about his disappearance add an additional layer of intrigue to his story. In the end, Ambrose Bierce's life and mysterious death remind us of the limits of our understanding and the enduring power of the unknown.

Chapter 25: The Mystery of the Somerton Man

The mystery of the Somerton Man, also known as the Tamam Shud case, is one of Australia's most enduring and perplexing unsolved cases. It began on December 1, 1948, when the body of an unidentified man was found on Somerton Beach, near Glenelg, a suburb of Adelaide, South Australia. Despite extensive investigations, the identity of the man and the circumstances surrounding his death remain unknown, fueling countless theories and speculations.

On the morning of December 1, 1948, John Lyons and his wife discovered a man lying on the sand, propped against the seawall with his legs extended and his feet crossed. At first, they assumed he was sleeping or intoxicated, but when they returned later and noticed he hadn't moved, they alerted the police. The man appeared to be in his mid-forties, dressed in a suit and tie, with polished shoes and no apparent signs of struggle or injury. His pockets contained several items, including a used bus ticket, an unused train ticket, a pack of cigarettes, matches, a comb, and a half-empty pack of chewing gum, but no identification.

The initial autopsy revealed that the man's heart was in good condition, and there were no signs of violence. However, his stomach contained blood, and the medical examiner concluded that the cause of death was likely poisoning, though no trace of any specific poison was found. The case was further complicated when a small scrap of paper was discovered in a hidden pocket of the man's trousers. The paper bore the words "Tamam Shud," which means "ended" or "finished" in Persian. This phrase comes from the final page of the Rubaiyat of Omar Khayyam, a collection of poems by the Persian poet.

This discovery led the police to search for the book from which the paper had been torn. Eventually, a copy of the Rubaiyat was found in the backseat of an unlocked car near the beach. The book contained a series of letters, believed to be a code, written on its back cover, as well as a phone number. The code, which has never been definitively deciphered, and the phone number provided the first real clues in the investigation.

The phone number belonged to a local nurse, Jessica "Jo" Thomson (née Harkness), who lived near Somerton Beach. When questioned by the police, she claimed not to know the dead man but appeared visibly distressed when shown a cast of his face. She later mentioned that she had once owned a copy of the Rubaiyat, which she had given to a man named Alfred Boxall. However, Boxall was found alive and well in Sydney, still in possession of the book, ruling him out as the Somerton Man.

The discovery of the book and the involvement of Jessica Thomson added layers of intrigue to the case. Some speculated that the Somerton Man was a spy, given the Cold War context and the mysterious code found in the book. Others theorized that he was involved in a love affair with Thomson, which led to his untimely death. However, without concrete evidence, these theories remained speculative.

In 1949, the body of the Somerton Man was embalmed and buried in West Terrace Cemetery, Adelaide. His identity remained a mystery, and the case gradually faded from public attention. However, the intrigue surrounding the case persisted, attracting the interest of amateur sleuths, researchers, and conspiracy theorists over the decades.

In the years following the discovery of the Somerton Man, several leads emerged, but none provided definitive answers. In the early 1950s, a man came forward claiming to have seen a similar-looking man in a photograph taken in Sydney. However, this lead also turned out to be a dead end. The cryptic code found in the Rubaiyat continued to baffle cryptographers and puzzle enthusiasts, with various attempts at decryption yielding no clear results.

The case received renewed attention in the 1990s when Professor Derek Abbott from the University of Adelaide began investigating the mystery. Abbott's research uncovered new details and rekindled public interest in the case. He examined the physical evidence, including the autopsy report and photographs, and interviewed surviving witnesses, including Jessica Thomson's family. His efforts to identify the Somerton Man included a detailed analysis of the code, genetic testing, and facial reconstruction.

One of Abbott's most intriguing discoveries was a potential connection between the Somerton Man and Jessica Thomson's son, Robin. Photographs of Robin revealed a rare genetic trait: his ear shape and a condition known as hypodontia, both of which matched those of the Somerton Man. This led to speculation that Robin could be the son of the Somerton Man, suggesting a deeper personal connection between Thomson and the unidentified man. Despite these findings, conclusive DNA evidence was not obtained at the time due to the degraded state of the Somerton Man's remains.

In recent years, advancements in forensic science and genetic testing have provided new opportunities to solve the case. In 2018, the South Australian government approved the exhumation of the Somerton Man's body for DNA analysis. The exhumation took place in May 2021, with the hope that modern technology could finally reveal his identity. The results of the DNA analysis are eagerly awaited by researchers and the public alike, as they may provide crucial clues to solving this long-standing mystery.

While the scientific investigation continues, various theories about the Somerton Man's identity and the circumstances of his death persist. Some believe he was a foreign spy, possibly Russian or British, given the context of the Cold War and the presence of the mysterious code. Others suggest he was a jilted lover or a victim of a crime of passion, linked to Jessica Thomson. There are also theories that he was involved in illegal activities, such as smuggling, which led to his demise.

The Somerton Man case has inspired numerous books, documentaries, and articles, each offering different perspectives and interpretations. It remains a popular topic for true crime enthusiasts and amateur detectives, who continue to explore the evidence and propose new theories. The enduring fascination with the case highlights the universal human desire to uncover the truth and solve the unknown.

As the investigation into the Somerton Man's identity progresses, the hope is that modern forensic techniques and genetic testing will finally provide answers to the questions that have lingered for over seventy years. The mystery of who he was, how he died, and the meaning of the cryptic "Tamam Shud" note may yet be resolved, bringing closure to one of Australia's most enigmatic cases.

Regardless of the outcome, the Somerton Man case serves as a reminder of the complexities and uncertainties of human life. It underscores the ways in which seemingly ordinary events can become the subject of enduring intrigue and speculation, capturing the imagination of generations. The Somerton Man, whoever he may have been, has become a symbol of the unknown, a testament to the enduring power of mystery and the human quest for understanding.

Chapter 26: The Mysterious Death of James Dean

The mysterious death of James Dean, one of Hollywood's most iconic and enigmatic figures, remains a topic of fascination and speculation more than six decades after the tragic event. James Byron Dean, born on February 8, 1931, in Marion, Indiana, achieved legendary status despite a brief film career that spanned only a few years and included just three major motion pictures: "East of Eden" (1955), "Rebel Without a Cause" (1955), and "Giant" (1956). His untimely death on September 30, 1955, at the age of 24, in a car accident has sparked numerous conspiracy theories and left a lasting impact on popular culture.

Dean's early life was marked by personal tragedy and a quest for identity. After his mother died when he was nine, Dean was sent to live with his aunt and uncle on their farm in Fairmount, Indiana. Despite the upheaval, he developed a passion for acting and eventually moved to California to pursue his dream. He attended UCLA, where he studied theater, and his talent quickly became evident. Dean's intense, brooding persona and naturalistic acting style resonated with audiences and garnered critical acclaim.

Dean's rise to stardom was meteoric. His portrayal of the troubled teenager Jim Stark in "Rebel Without a Cause" made him a cultural icon, embodying the restless youth of the 1950s. His performances in "East of Eden" and "Giant" further solidified his reputation as a gifted actor capable of conveying deep emotional complexity. However, Dean's personal life was tumultuous. He had a reputation for being moody and difficult, and his relationships with friends and lovers were often strained.

Dean's passion for fast cars and racing was well-known. He owned several high-performance vehicles, including a Porsche 356 Speedster and a Triumph motorcycle. In early 1955, he purchased a Porsche 550 Spyder, which he nicknamed "Little Bastard." This car would become inextricably linked to his fate. Dean planned to race the Spyder in an event in Salinas, California, on October 1, 1955. Accompanied by his mechanic, Rolf Wütherich, he set out on a drive to break in the new car and prepare for the race.

On the afternoon of September 30, 1955, Dean and Wütherich left Los Angeles and headed north on U.S. Route 466. Around 5:45 p.m., near the junction of Route 466 and Route 41 in Cholame, California, their journey took a fatal turn. A 1950 Ford Tudor, driven by 23-year-old college student Donald Turnupseed, made a left turn across Dean's path. Unable to avoid the collision, Dean's Porsche collided almost head-on with the Ford. The impact was devastating. Dean suffered severe injuries, including a broken neck and multiple internal injuries, and was pronounced dead on arrival at the Paso Robles War Memorial Hospital. Wütherich was thrown from the car and survived, though he sustained serious injuries.

The sudden and violent nature of Dean's death shocked the world. He had been on the cusp of superstardom, and his demise was a profound loss to Hollywood and his legions of fans. The incident immediately gave rise to numerous rumors and conspiracy theories. Some speculated that Dean had a death wish or that the crash was somehow staged. Others suggested that "Little Bastard" was cursed, pointing to a series of subsequent accidents involving parts from the wrecked car.

The legend of the "curse" of James Dean's car began with George Barris, a custom car designer who purchased the wreckage of the Porsche. According to Barris, the car exhibited an uncanny tendency to cause accidents and misfortune. He claimed that while the wreckage was being transported, the truck carrying it slipped off its trailer and injured a mechanic. Further incidents included another accident involving a driver who used parts from the Porsche in his own car, which resulted in a fatal crash. While these stories have been widely publicized, many are difficult to verify and have taken on a life of their own as part of the James Dean mythos.

Beyond the supposed curse, other aspects of Dean's death have invited scrutiny. Some researchers have suggested that the official accounts of the crash may not tell the full story. Questions have been raised about the speed at which Dean was driving, whether he was wearing his seatbelt, and the exact circumstances of the collision. These inquiries have been fueled by inconsistencies in eyewitness testimonies and reports from the scene. However, despite these lingering doubts, no definitive evidence has emerged to contradict the accepted narrative.

Dean's death also had a significant impact on automobile safety awareness. The widespread coverage of the crash and the subsequent public reaction underscored the dangers of reckless driving and the need for safer driving practices. Dean himself had participated in a public service announcement shortly before his death, warning against speeding with the ironic closing line, "The life you save might be mine." This tragic twist added another layer to the legend surrounding his death.

In the years following his death, James Dean's legacy has only grown. He became an enduring symbol of youthful rebellion and the fleeting nature of life. His influence can be seen in various aspects of popular culture, from fashion to music to film. Many actors and artists cite Dean as a profound inspiration, drawn to his raw emotional intensity and his ability to convey vulnerability and defiance.

Dean's three major films have achieved classic status and continue to be studied and admired for their groundbreaking performances and themes. "Rebel Without a Cause" remains a defining portrayal of teenage angst and disillusionment, while "East of Eden" and "Giant" showcase Dean's range and depth as an actor. Posthumously, Dean received two Academy Award nominations for Best Actor, making him the first actor to receive multiple nominations after death.

In addition to his films, Dean's persona has been immortalized in numerous biographies, documentaries, and fictional works. His life and death have been the subject of extensive analysis, and he has been depicted in various forms of media, from books to stage plays to television series. His enduring appeal lies in the combination of his undeniable talent, his tragic and untimely death, and the aura of mystery that continues to surround him.

The impact of James Dean's death also extends to the world of motorsports. His passion for racing and his tragic end have made him a poignant figure in the history of automotive culture. Dean's love for speed and his involvement in the racing community have been commemorated in car shows, races, and automotive memorabilia. His Porsche 550 Spyder, "Little Bastard," has become one of the most infamous cars in history, symbolizing both the thrill and the peril of the pursuit of speed.

James Dean's legacy is a testament to the enduring power of myth and the human fascination with figures who burn brightly and leave an indelible mark on the world. His life story, marked by ambition, talent, and tragedy, continues to resonate with new generations, ensuring that his memory remains vibrant and compelling. The mystery and speculation surrounding his death add to the aura of his legend, inviting ongoing exploration and reflection.

As we continue to celebrate and examine the life and death of James Dean, it is important to recognize the complexities and contradictions that made him such a compelling figure. He was a talented actor and a passionate individual who lived life on his own terms, embodying the spirit of rebellion and authenticity. His untimely death serves as a poignant reminder of the fragility of life and the enduring impact that a single individual can have on culture and history.

The mysterious death of James Dean, therefore, remains a powerful and evocative chapter in the annals of Hollywood lore. It underscores the unpredictable nature of life and the way in which certain figures capture the collective imagination. Dean's legacy is not just one of cinematic achievement, but also of the enduring human fascination with those who live boldly and leave behind an unforgettable legacy.

Chapter 27: The Assassination of Malcolm X

The assassination of Malcolm X, a pivotal figure in the American Civil Rights Movement, remains one of the most complex and debated events in modern history. Malcolm X, born Malcolm Little on May 19, 1925, in Omaha, Nebraska, rose to prominence as a charismatic and controversial leader who advocated for the rights of African Americans. His life was marked by a profound transformation from a street hustler to a prominent spokesperson for the Nation of Islam (NOI) and, eventually, an independent human rights activist. The circumstances surrounding his assassination on February 21, 1965, are shrouded in controversy, involving allegations of government conspiracy, internal strife within the NOI, and broader societal tensions.

Malcolm X's early life was fraught with hardship. His father, Earl Little, was a Baptist preacher and an ardent supporter of Marcus Garvey's Universal Negro Improvement Association, which promoted black self-reliance and unity. Earl's activism made the Little family a target of white supremacist groups like the Ku Klux Klan. When Malcolm was six, his father was killed in what was officially ruled a streetcar accident, though Malcolm and his family believed it was a murder orchestrated by white supremacists. His mother, Louise Little, struggled to keep the family together and eventually suffered a mental breakdown, leading to her institutionalization. Consequently, Malcolm and his siblings were placed in foster homes.

These early experiences of racial violence and family disintegration profoundly shaped Malcolm's worldview. As a teenager, he drifted into a life of crime in Boston and New York City, earning the nickname "Detroit Red" for his reddish hair. In 1946, he was arrested for burglary and sentenced to ten years in prison. During his incarceration, Malcolm underwent a significant transformation. He educated himself by reading extensively and became a devoted follower of the Nation of Islam, a religious and political organization that combined elements of traditional Islam with black nationalist ideology. Upon his release in 1952, he adopted the surname "X" to symbolize the loss of his African ancestry and heritage, which he argued had been obliterated by slavery.

Under the mentorship of Elijah Muhammad, the leader of the Nation of Islam, Malcolm X quickly rose through the ranks to become the organization's most prominent spokesperson. His oratory skills, charisma, and uncompromising stance on racial issues garnered him a large following. He was a vocal critic of the mainstream civil rights movement's emphasis on nonviolence and integration, advocating instead for black self-defense and separatism. Malcolm's rhetoric was often inflammatory, as he condemned white America for its systemic racism and oppression of black people.

Despite his loyalty to Elijah Muhammad, Malcolm X's relationship with the NOI began to fray in the early 1960s. He became increasingly disillusioned with Muhammad's leadership and moral conduct, particularly upon discovering that Muhammad had engaged in extramarital affairs with several of his secretaries, fathering multiple children. Malcolm's public announcement of these transgressions created a rift within the organization. Additionally, his political views were evolving. After a pilgrimage to Mecca in 1964, Malcolm converted to Sunni Islam and adopted the name El-Hajj Malik El-Shabazz. The pilgrimage broadened his perspective, leading him to advocate for racial unity and international human rights, rather than just black nationalism.

Malcolm X's departure from the NOI and his subsequent establishment of the Muslim Mosque, Inc., and the Organization of Afro-American Unity (OAAU) marked a new chapter in his activism. He sought to address racial issues on a global scale, connecting the struggles of African Americans with those of oppressed peoples worldwide. However, his break from the NOI intensified the animosity between him and his former associates. Malcolm received numerous death threats, and tensions escalated as his influence grew.

On February 21, 1965, Malcolm X was scheduled to speak at the Audubon Ballroom in Harlem, New York City. As he began his address, a disturbance broke out in the audience. In the ensuing chaos, three men rushed the stage and fired multiple shots at Malcolm, striking him several times. He was pronounced dead on arrival at Columbia Presbyterian Hospital. The autopsy revealed 21 gunshot wounds to his chest, left shoulder, arms, and legs. The assassination shocked the nation and sent ripples through the civil rights movement.

Three men were arrested and convicted for Malcolm X's murder: Talmadge Hayer (also known as Thomas Hagan), Norman 3X Butler (later known as Muhammad Abdul Aziz), and Thomas 15X Johnson (later known as Khalil Islam). Hayer, who was apprehended at the scene, confessed to the crime but insisted that Butler and Johnson were innocent. Despite his testimony, all three men were convicted and sentenced to life imprisonment. In the decades that followed, doubts about the fairness and accuracy of the investigation and trial persisted.

Numerous theories have emerged regarding the true motives and perpetrators behind Malcolm X's assassination. Some researchers and historians argue that internal strife within the Nation of Islam was a significant factor. Malcolm's outspoken criticism of Elijah Muhammad and his departure from the NOI were seen as acts of betrayal, leading to deep resentment among some members. The organization had a history of using violent means to silence dissenters, and many believe that Malcolm's murder was orchestrated by high-ranking officials within the NOI.

Others speculate that government agencies, particularly the FBI and the New York Police Department (NYPD), were involved in or had prior knowledge of the assassination plot. The FBI's COINTELPRO (Counter Intelligence Program) targeted civil rights activists and organizations, including Malcolm X and the NOI, with the aim of disrupting and discrediting their activities. Declassified documents have revealed that both the FBI and the NYPD had infiltrated the NOI and were monitoring Malcolm closely. Some theorists suggest that these agencies either facilitated the assassination or deliberately failed to prevent it, seeing Malcolm as a threat to national security and social stability.

In 2021, the case took a significant turn when Manhattan District Attorney Cyrus Vance Jr. announced that his office would review the convictions of Butler and Johnson. This decision came after the release of the documentary series "Who Killed Malcolm X?" which raised serious questions about the original investigation and trial. The documentary highlighted inconsistencies in the prosecution's case and presented new evidence suggesting that Butler and Johnson were wrongfully convicted. In November 2021, both men were exonerated, with the court acknowledging that the prosecution had withheld evidence that could have proven their innocence.

The exoneration of Butler and Johnson has renewed calls for a comprehensive re-examination of Malcolm X's assassination. Activists and scholars argue that a full accounting of the events leading up to his death is necessary to uncover the truth and achieve justice. This includes investigating the roles of the NOI, the FBI, and other potential actors in the assassination plot.

Malcolm X's legacy continues to inspire and challenge people around the world. His journey from a troubled youth to a visionary leader who advocated for justice, equality, and human rights resonates with contemporary struggles against racism and oppression. His autobiography, co-authored with Alex Haley, remains a seminal work, offering insights into his life, beliefs, and the broader civil rights movement. His speeches and writings continue to be studied and celebrated for their eloquence, passion, and radical vision.

The unresolved questions surrounding Malcolm X's assassination highlight the broader historical context of political violence and state surveillance against activists and leaders who challenge the status quo. His death is part of a tragic pattern that includes the assassinations of other prominent figures of the era, such as Martin Luther King Jr. and Robert F. Kennedy. These events underscore the high stakes and profound risks faced by those who dare to confront entrenched systems of power and injustice.

As we reflect on Malcolm X's life and legacy, it is crucial to recognize his contributions to the struggle for civil rights and human dignity. His transformation from Malcolm Little to Malcolm X to El-Hajj Malik El-Shabazz embodies a journey of self-discovery, resilience, and unwavering commitment to justice. His call for black empowerment, self-determination, and international solidarity remains relevant today, as movements for racial and social justice continue to draw inspiration from his example.

The assassination of Malcolm X is not just a historical event; it is a reminder of the ongoing fight for truth, accountability, and justice. It challenges us to critically examine the past, honor the sacrifices of those who came before us, and continue the work of building a more just and equitable world. The pursuit of justice for Malcolm X, and for all those who have suffered similar fates, is an essential part of this ongoing struggle.

Chapter 28: The Enigma of the Bermuda Triangle

The Bermuda Triangle, also known as the Devil's Triangle, is a loosely defined region in the western part of the North Atlantic Ocean, covering an area of approximately 500,000 square miles. The vertices of this triangle are generally accepted to be Miami, Florida; San Juan, Puerto Rico; and the island of Bermuda. This area has been the subject of numerous myths, legends, and speculative theories due to the mysterious disappearances of ships and aircraft that have been reported since the mid-20th century. Despite extensive investigations and scientific explanations, the enigma of the Bermuda Triangle continues to capture the public imagination, fueled by accounts of unexplained phenomena, strange occurrences, and the sheer volume of incidents attributed to this region.

The intrigue surrounding the Bermuda Triangle began to gain significant traction in the 1950s. One of the earliest and most famous cases involved Flight 19, a group of five U.S. Navy Avenger torpedo bombers that disappeared during a training mission on December 5, 1945. The flight, led by Lieutenant Charles Taylor, took off from Fort Lauderdale, Florida, but soon encountered navigational difficulties. The radio transmissions from the flight crew indicated that they were disoriented and could not determine their position. Despite efforts to guide them back to base, contact was eventually lost. A rescue mission consisting of a PBM Mariner seaplane was dispatched, but this aircraft also vanished, adding to the mystery. No trace of Flight 19 or the rescue plane was ever found, leading to widespread speculation and the birth of the Bermuda Triangle legend.

Over the years, many other ships and aircraft have reportedly disappeared under mysterious circumstances within the Bermuda Triangle. Some of these include the USS Cyclops, a Navy cargo ship that vanished in March 1918 with 309 crew members on board, and the SS Marine Sulphur Queen, a tanker carrying molten sulfur that disappeared in February 1963. The unexplained loss of these vessels, along with numerous smaller incidents, has fueled theories ranging from natural phenomena to extraterrestrial involvement.

One of the most compelling explanations for the Bermuda Triangle's mysteries involves environmental and geographical factors. The region is known for its unpredictable weather patterns, including sudden storms and waterspouts, which can pose significant dangers to ships and aircraft. Additionally, the area is situated along the Gulf Stream, a powerful ocean current that can rapidly change weather conditions and create treacherous sea states. The combination of these factors can easily lead to accidents and disappearances, especially during the era before modern navigation and communication technologies.

Another natural explanation focuses on the presence of methane hydrates on the ocean floor. Methane hydrates are crystalline structures that trap methane gas within a lattice of water molecules. It has been proposed that disturbances to the seafloor, such as seismic activity, could release large amounts of methane gas, causing the water to become less dense and reducing buoyancy. This phenomenon, known as a "methane hydrate blowout," could theoretically cause ships to sink rapidly without warning. However, there is limited evidence to support this theory, and it remains speculative.

Magnetic anomalies have also been suggested as a possible cause of the strange occurrences in the Bermuda Triangle. Some theories posit that the region is home to unusual magnetic fields that interfere with navigation instruments, leading to disorientation and loss of direction. While it is true that the Bermuda Triangle is one of the few places on Earth where magnetic north and true north align, known as agonic lines, this alignment alone is unlikely to cause the widespread disruptions suggested by the theory. Modern navigation systems are designed to account for such variations, further diminishing the likelihood of magnetic anomalies as a primary cause.

The human element plays a significant role in many of the incidents attributed to the Bermuda Triangle. Human error, equipment failure, and poor decision-making are common factors in maritime and aviation accidents. In the case of Flight 19, for example, it is believed that navigational errors by Lieutenant Taylor, combined with a lack of fuel and deteriorating weather conditions, contributed to the loss of the aircraft. Similarly, many of the shipwrecks and disappearances in the region can be attributed to human factors rather than mysterious forces.

Despite these plausible explanations, the allure of the Bermuda Triangle persists, bolstered by sensationalized accounts and media coverage. Books, documentaries, and movies have perpetuated the myth, often emphasizing the more fantastical theories. These include suggestions of alien abductions, time warps, underwater alien bases, and the influence of the lost city of Atlantis. While these ideas make for compelling storytelling, they lack credible evidence and scientific support.

One of the key figures in popularizing the Bermuda Triangle mystery was Charles Berlitz, an author and linguist who wrote extensively on paranormal phenomena. His 1974 book, "The Bermuda Triangle," compiled various accounts of disappearances and proposed a range of supernatural explanations. Berlitz's work was instrumental in bringing the Bermuda Triangle to the attention of a global audience, but it was also criticized for its lack of rigorous investigation and reliance on anecdotal evidence.

The scientific community has largely dismissed the more outlandish theories associated with the Bermuda Triangle, focusing instead on empirical evidence and rational explanations. The U.S. Coast Guard and other maritime agencies have pointed out that the number of incidents in the Bermuda Triangle is not significantly higher than in other heavily traveled regions of the world. Additionally, advances in technology and improved safety measures have reduced the frequency of accidents, further undermining the notion of a mysterious phenomenon at work.

However, the Bermuda Triangle remains a subject of fascination and curiosity. It represents a modern myth, a space where science and speculation intersect, and where the unknown continues to captivate the human imagination. The enduring mystery of the Bermuda Triangle speaks to a deeper cultural and psychological need to explore and understand the unexplainable. It taps into our innate sense of wonder and our desire to find meaning in the face of uncertainty.

In recent years, the Bermuda Triangle has become a popular destination for tourists and adventurers seeking to experience the mystery firsthand. Cruises, flights, and expeditions offer a chance to explore the region and learn about its history and lore. While these ventures often emphasize the romantic and mysterious aspects of the Bermuda Triangle, they also provide opportunities for education and scientific inquiry.

Researchers continue to study the environmental and geological characteristics of the Bermuda Triangle, seeking to better understand the natural forces at play. Advances in oceanography, meteorology, and geology have provided valuable insights into the dynamics of the region. For example, studies of underwater topography have revealed the presence of deep trenches, underwater volcanoes, and other geological features that could contribute to the area's hazardous conditions. Similarly, ongoing research into atmospheric phenomena and ocean currents helps to explain the sudden and severe weather changes that are common in the Bermuda Triangle.

Despite the wealth of scientific knowledge, the Bermuda Triangle retains its enigmatic allure. It is a reminder that, even in an age of technological advancement and scientific discovery, there are still mysteries that elude our understanding. The Bermuda Triangle challenges us to question our assumptions, explore the unknown, and remain open to the possibility that some phenomena may never be fully explained.

The enduring fascination with the Bermuda Triangle also highlights the interplay between science, culture, and media. The way we perceive and interpret unexplained events is influenced by a complex web of factors, including historical context, cultural narratives, and media representation. The Bermuda Triangle serves as a case study in how myths are created, sustained, and transformed over time, reflecting broader societal concerns and interests.

As we continue to explore the mysteries of the Bermuda Triangle, it is important to balance curiosity with critical thinking. The region offers a rich tapestry of stories and phenomena that can inspire both wonder and skepticism. By approaching the Bermuda Triangle with an open mind and a commitment to evidence-based inquiry, we can deepen our understanding of this fascinating enigma and the broader natural world.

Chapter 29: The Mysterious Passing of Jimi Hendrix

Jimi Hendrix, born Johnny Allen Hendrix on November 27, 1942, in Seattle, Washington, is widely regarded as one of the greatest guitarists in the history of rock music. Hendrix's innovative style, technical proficiency, and expressive performances revolutionized the electric guitar's role in popular music. His career, though tragically short-lived, left an indelible mark on the music world, influencing countless musicians across genres. The circumstances surrounding his death on September 18, 1970, remain a source of speculation, controversy, and mystery, adding another layer to his enigmatic legacy.

Hendrix's early life was marked by instability and hardship. His parents, Al Hendrix and Lucille Jeter, had a tumultuous relationship, and Hendrix experienced a series of relocations and family disruptions during his childhood. Despite these challenges, he developed a deep passion for music, teaching himself to play the guitar and drawing inspiration from blues, jazz, and rock influences. By the early 1960s, Hendrix had established himself as a talented and sought-after session guitarist, working with artists such as Little Richard, The Isley Brothers, and Curtis Knight.

Hendrix's breakthrough came in 1966 when he moved to London and formed The Jimi Hendrix Experience with bassist Noel Redding and drummer Mitch Mitchell. The trio's debut album, "Are You Experienced" (1967), was a critical and commercial success, featuring iconic tracks such as "Purple Haze," "Hey Joe," and "The Wind Cries Mary." Hendrix's innovative use of feedback, distortion, and wah-wah effects, combined with his virtuosic playing and charismatic stage presence, set him apart as a revolutionary force in rock music.

Over the next few years, Hendrix released several more critically acclaimed albums, including "Axis: Bold as Love" (1967) and "Electric

Ladyland" (1968). His performances at major music festivals, such as the Monterey Pop Festival and Woodstock, further cemented his status as a legendary performer. However, Hendrix's rapid rise to fame was accompanied by intense personal and professional pressures, leading to struggles with substance abuse, legal issues, and strained relationships with bandmates and management.

In the months leading up to his death, Hendrix's life was marked by increasing turbulence and uncertainty. He was in the midst of a grueling tour schedule, working on new music, and navigating complex legal and financial disputes. His personal life was also complicated, with a series of romantic entanglements and a growing dependency on drugs and alcohol. Despite these challenges, Hendrix continued to create and perform, showcasing his enduring talent and dedication to his craft.

On September 17, 1970, Hendrix spent the evening with Monika Dannemann, a German figure skater and artist whom he had been dating. The couple stayed at Dannemann's apartment in the Samarkand Hotel in London. According to Dannemann, Hendrix took some sleeping pills to help him rest, as he had been struggling with insomnia. The details of the events that followed are murky and have been the subject of much speculation and debate.

On the morning of September 18, 1970, Dannemann found Hendrix unresponsive and called for an ambulance. Hendrix was transported to St. Mary Abbot's Hospital, where he was pronounced dead. The official cause of death was asphyxia due to aspiration of vomit, resulting from barbiturate intoxication. Specifically, Hendrix had taken nine Vesparax tablets, a powerful sedative prescribed for severe insomnia. The dosage was 18 times the recommended amount, leading to a fatal overdose.

The circumstances surrounding Hendrix's death have given rise to numerous theories and controversies. Some have suggested that his death was accidental, a tragic result of his struggle with insomnia and reliance on prescription medication. Others have speculated that it was a suicide, citing his tumultuous personal life, professional pressures, and alleged expressions of despair in the days leading up to his death. However, those close to Hendrix have often disputed this notion, arguing that he was looking forward to future projects and had not exhibited suicidal tendencies.

One of the most persistent and controversial theories is that Hendrix was murdered. Various accounts have implicated different individuals, including Monika Dannemann, his manager Michael Jeffery, and even government agencies. Some proponents of this theory argue that Hendrix's death was orchestrated to gain control of his lucrative music catalog or to silence his politically and socially charged voice. Dannemann, in particular, has been the subject of intense scrutiny. Her inconsistent statements and behavior in the aftermath of Hendrix's death have fueled suspicions, though no concrete evidence has emerged to support these allegations.

Michael Jeffery, Hendrix's manager, has also been a figure of interest in conspiracy theories. Jeffery was known for his unscrupulous business practices and had a contentious relationship with Hendrix. Some have suggested that Jeffery, facing financial difficulties and fearing that Hendrix was planning to terminate their business relationship, may have had a motive to orchestrate his death. Again, while these theories are intriguing, they remain speculative and unsupported by definitive proof.

Adding to the mystery are the discrepancies in the accounts of Hendrix's final hours. For example, there are conflicting reports about the timeline of events and the actions taken by those present. Dannemann's statements have varied over the years, and some witnesses have suggested that Hendrix was alive when the ambulance arrived, contrary to the official account. These inconsistencies have fueled ongoing debates and investigations into the true nature of Hendrix's death.

The medical response to Hendrix's condition has also been questioned. Some have argued that the emergency medical team and hospital staff may have failed to provide adequate care or misjudged the severity of his condition. The chaotic and unclear nature of the response has left many wondering if more could have been done to save his life.

In the decades since Hendrix's death, new information and perspectives have continued to emerge, further complicating the narrative. For instance, in 2009, James "Tappy" Wright, a former roadie for Hendrix, published a memoir in which he claimed that Michael Jeffery confessed to having Hendrix killed to collect on a life insurance policy. This explosive allegation reignited interest in the murder theory, though it has been met with skepticism and criticism from other Hendrix associates and biographers.

The impact of Jimi Hendrix's death on the music world cannot be overstated. His loss was a devastating blow to the artistic community and his countless fans. Hendrix was not only a pioneering musician but also a cultural icon who pushed the boundaries of what was possible with the electric guitar. His influence can be seen in the work of countless artists who followed in his footsteps, and his recordings continue to inspire new generations of musicians and listeners.

In the wake of his passing, numerous posthumous albums and compilations have been released, showcasing Hendrix's unreleased material and live performances. These recordings have provided further insight into his creative process and the depth of his musical genius. Efforts to preserve and celebrate Hendrix's legacy have included the establishment of the Jimi Hendrix Experience Museum and the Hendrix family estate's ongoing efforts to protect his intellectual property and promote his music.

Despite the efforts to honor and remember Hendrix, the unresolved questions surrounding his death continue to cast a shadow over his legacy. The various theories and speculations reflect broader themes of distrust, intrigue, and the search for truth that often accompany the deaths of influential public figures. The enduring mystery of Hendrix's passing serves as a reminder of the complex interplay between fame, personal struggle, and the unpredictable nature of life and death.

Jimi Hendrix's story is one of extraordinary talent, innovation, and a life cut tragically short. His music remains a testament to his genius, and his influence endures in the hearts and minds of those who continue to be moved by his work. The mystery of his death adds a layer of poignancy to his legacy, inviting ongoing reflection and exploration of the many facets of his remarkable life. As we continue to celebrate Hendrix's contributions to music and culture, we are also reminded of the fragility of human existence and the enduring quest for understanding and meaning in the face of the unknown.

Chapter 30: The Unsolved Murder of Tupac Shakur

The unsolved murder of Tupac Shakur is one of the most enduring mysteries in the world of music and popular culture. Tupac Amaru Shakur, known professionally as 2Pac, was a highly influential rapper, actor, and activist. Born on June 16, 1971, in East Harlem, New York City, Shakur rose to prominence in the early 1990s with his provocative lyrics, charismatic persona, and powerful social commentary. His music addressed a range of issues, including racial inequality, police brutality, poverty, and the struggles of inner-city life. Despite his immense talent and success, Tupac's life was marked by controversy and violence, culminating in his untimely death at the age of 25.

On the night of September 7, 1996, Tupac Shakur attended the Mike Tyson-Bruce Seldon boxing match at the MGM Grand in Las Vegas, Nevada. After the fight, he was involved in a physical altercation with Orlando Anderson, a member of the Southside Crips gang, in the casino lobby. This incident is believed to have been a catalyst for the events that followed. Later that evening, Shakur and his entourage, including Death Row Records CEO Marion "Suge" Knight, left the MGM Grand in a convoy of cars. Shakur was riding in the passenger seat of a black BMW 750iL driven by Knight.

At approximately 11:15 PM, as they were stopped at a red light at the intersection of East Flamingo Road and Koval Lane, a white Cadillac pulled up alongside the BMW. The occupants of the Cadillac opened fire, striking Shakur multiple times. He was hit in the chest, pelvis, and right hand and thigh. Suge Knight, who was grazed by a bullet fragment, managed to drive away from the scene, eventually being flagged down by police and taken to University Medical Center of Southern Nevada. Despite extensive medical efforts, Tupac Shakur succumbed to his injuries six days later, on September 13, 1996. His death shocked the world and left an indelible mark on the music industry.

The investigation into Tupac Shakur's murder was plagued by numerous challenges and controversies from the outset. The Las Vegas Metropolitan Police Department (LVMPD) faced criticism for their handling of the case, including allegations of procedural errors, lack of cooperation from witnesses, and potential bias. One of the key difficulties was the "no-snitch" culture prevalent in the hip-hop community and among those associated with gang activity, which hindered the flow of information and cooperation with law enforcement.

One of the primary suspects in the case was Orlando Anderson, the man involved in the altercation with Shakur at the MGM Grand. Anderson, a known member of the Southside Crips, was questioned by police but denied any involvement in the shooting. He was never formally charged, and the case against him was largely circumstantial. Anderson himself was murdered in an unrelated gang shooting in May 1998, further complicating the investigation.

Another significant aspect of the case revolves around the East Coast-West Coast rivalry that dominated the hip-hop scene in the 1990s. Tupac Shakur was closely associated with the West Coast and Death Row Records, while The Notorious B.I.G. (Christopher Wallace), a prominent East Coast rapper, was affiliated with Bad Boy Records. The rivalry between the two labels, and by extension their respective coasts, was fueled by a series of public feuds, diss tracks, and violent incidents. This animosity was seen by many as a contributing factor to Shakur's murder.

In the years following Tupac's death, various theories and conspiracy claims have emerged, adding layers of complexity and intrigue to the case. Some believe that Suge Knight orchestrated the murder, motivated by business disputes or fears that Shakur was planning to leave Death Row Records. Knight, who was present at the scene and survived the shooting, has consistently denied any involvement. Others suggest that the murder was a result of a gang-related retaliation or part of a larger conspiracy involving corrupt law enforcement officials and rival music industry figures.

One of the most persistent conspiracy theories is that Tupac Shakur faked his own death and is living in hiding. This theory is fueled by the numerous posthumous album releases, sightings, and cryptic messages in his music and interviews. Despite the lack of credible evidence supporting this claim, it remains a popular narrative among some fans and conspiracy enthusiasts.

Over the years, several investigative efforts have sought to uncover the truth behind Tupac's murder. Notable among these is the work of former LAPD detective Russell Poole, who investigated both the Shakur and Wallace murders. Poole developed a theory that implicated Suge Knight and corrupt LAPD officers in a broader criminal conspiracy. His findings were the basis for journalist Randall Sullivan's book "LAbyrinth" and the subsequent film adaptation, "City of Lies," starring Johnny Depp as Poole. Despite Poole's extensive investigation, his theory remains contentious and has not led to any legal resolution.

In 2002, journalist and filmmaker Nick Broomfield released the documentary "Biggie & Tupac," which explored the murders of both rappers. Broomfield's film presented interviews with key figures, including former Death Row employees and associates, and highlighted the potential involvement of law enforcement in the cover-up of the crimes. The documentary raised important questions but did not provide definitive answers.

More recently, the true crime television series "Unsolved: The Murders of Tupac and The Notorious B.I.G." aired in 2018, dramatizing the investigations into the murders of the two iconic rappers. The series, based on the real-life work of LAPD detective Greg Kading, offered a fresh perspective on the cases. Kading's investigation, detailed in his book "Murder Rap," proposed that Orlando Anderson was responsible for Tupac's murder and that Wallace's murder was a retaliation orchestrated by Suge Knight. Kading's findings have been influential but remain a subject of debate and controversy.

Despite the passage of nearly three decades, the murder of Tupac Shakur remains officially unsolved. The lack of resolution has perpetuated a sense of injustice and frustration among his family, friends, and fans. Tupac's mother, Afeni Shakur, who was a prominent figure in the Black Panther Party and a steadfast advocate for her son's legacy, dedicated much of her life to seeking justice for Tupac. Afeni passed away in 2016, without seeing her son's murder solved.

Tupac Shakur's legacy extends far beyond his untimely death. He is remembered as a prolific artist who used his platform to speak out against social injustices and advocate for change. His music continues to resonate with audiences worldwide, addressing themes that remain relevant today. Tracks like "Changes," "Dear Mama," and "Keep Ya Head Up" are celebrated for their powerful messages and emotional depth. Tupac's influence can be seen in the work of countless contemporary artists who cite him as an inspiration.

In addition to his musical contributions, Tupac was a talented actor, appearing in films such as "Juice," "Poetic Justice," and "Gridlock'd." His performances showcased his versatility and charisma, further solidifying his status as a cultural icon. Tupac's impact on popular culture is evident in the continued interest in his life and legacy, as well as the numerous books, documentaries, and films dedicated to exploring his story.

The unsolved murder of Tupac Shakur has also had a lasting impact on the music industry and the broader hip-hop community. It highlighted the violence and volatility that plagued the scene during the 1990s, prompting calls for unity and peace among artists and fans. The tragic loss of such a gifted and influential figure underscored the need for addressing the root causes of violence and fostering a more positive and supportive environment within the industry.

In recent years, there have been renewed calls for a thorough re-examination of Tupac's murder case. Advances in forensic science, coupled with new information and perspectives, offer the potential for uncovering new leads and evidence. The persistence of journalists, investigators, and fans dedicated to seeking the truth keeps the hope alive that one day, justice may be served.

As the mystery of Tupac Shakur's murder endures, so too does his enduring legacy. He remains an emblem of artistic brilliance, resilience, and the enduring power of music to effect change. His life and career, marked by triumph and tragedy, continue to inspire and provoke thought, ensuring that Tupac Shakur will never be forgotten. The quest for answers and justice in his case serves as a reminder of the complexities and challenges inherent in the pursuit of truth and the need for continued vigilance in addressing unsolved crimes.

The story of Tupac Shakur is a poignant testament to the transformative power of art and the enduring quest for justice. His music and message live on, echoing through the generations and serving as a beacon of hope and inspiration. As we remember Tupac and his contributions to the world, we also honor the enduring spirit of those who continue to seek the truth and fight for justice in his name. The unresolved nature of his murder serves as a stark reminder of the work that remains to be done, but it also underscores the lasting impact of his legacy on the world.

Chapter 31: The Disappearance of Agatha Christie

The disappearance of Agatha Christie in December 1926 is one of the most intriguing mysteries in literary history, capturing the imagination of the public and leaving a legacy that endures to this day. Agatha Christie, born on September 15, 1890, in Torquay, England, was already a well-known mystery writer by the time of her disappearance, having published several successful novels featuring her iconic detective characters, Hercule Poirot and Miss Marple. Her sudden and unexplained disappearance at the age of 36 sparked a nationwide search and generated widespread speculation and media frenzy.

On the evening of December 3, 1926, Agatha Christie left her home, Styles, in Sunningdale, Berkshire, after an argument with her husband, Colonel Archibald Christie. The couple's marriage had been under significant strain due to Archibald's infidelity with a woman named Nancy Neele, and Agatha's emotional state was further compounded by the recent death of her mother, Clara. The stresses of her personal life, combined with the pressures of her successful writing career, created a tumultuous environment.

Agatha Christie left a note for her secretary, stating that she was going to Yorkshire, but did not provide specific details about her plans. She then drove her car, a Morris Cowley, towards London. Early the next morning, her abandoned car was discovered at Newlands Corner, near Guildford in Surrey. The car was found with an expired driving license and clothes inside, but there was no sign of Agatha herself. This discovery prompted immediate concern and initiated a massive search operation involving police, volunteers, and even airplanes.

The search for Agatha Christie quickly became a national sensation, with newspapers across Britain and beyond covering the story extensively. The press speculated wildly about the reasons for her disappearance, with theories ranging from amnesia and suicide to an elaborate publicity stunt or a real-life mystery plot concocted by the author herself. The involvement of her fellow writers, including Sir Arthur Conan Doyle, who consulted a medium to locate her, and Dorothy L. Sayers, who visited the scene of the disappearance, only added to the drama and intrigue.

During the search, more than 1,000 police officers and 15,000 volunteers combed the surrounding countryside, while reservoirs and ponds were dredged in the hope of finding clues. Despite these extensive efforts, there were few leads, and the mystery deepened as days turned into weeks. The disappearance captivated the public's imagination, and the pressure to find Agatha Christie intensified.

The breakthrough in the case came on December 14, 1926, when Agatha Christie was discovered staying at the Swan Hydropathic Hotel (now the Old Swan Hotel) in Harrogate, Yorkshire, under the name Theresa Neele. She had registered at the hotel on December 4, the day after her disappearance, and had been staying there for 11 days. During her time at the hotel, she seemed to be suffering from amnesia and did not recognize herself as the famous author Agatha Christie. Hotel staff described her as being in a "dazed and confused" state, although she participated in social activities, including dancing and reading newspapers that covered her own disappearance.

Agatha Christie's husband, Archibald, traveled to Harrogate to bring her home. Upon being reunited with him, she reportedly showed no recognition of him initially but gradually began to regain her memory. The details of her disappearance and her state of mind during those 11 days remain unclear, as Agatha Christie herself never provided a full explanation. She later stated that she had suffered a complete mental breakdown brought on by a combination of personal and professional stresses, which had resulted in a temporary loss of memory and identity.

The mystery of Agatha Christie's disappearance has inspired numerous books, documentaries, and fictionalized accounts, as well as continued speculation and debate among biographers and scholars. Some suggest that her disappearance was a cry for help or an attempt to escape the pressures of her life, while others believe it may have been a calculated act to humiliate her husband and draw attention to his infidelity. There are also those who argue that the incident was a genuine case of fugue state or dissociative amnesia, a rare condition often triggered by severe psychological trauma.

In her autobiography, published posthumously in 1977, Agatha Christie made only a brief reference to her disappearance, stating that she had no memory of the events that transpired during those days. This lack of detailed explanation has only fueled further speculation and left the door open for various interpretations of what might have happened.

The impact of Agatha Christie's disappearance on her career and legacy was significant. Despite the personal turmoil she experienced, she continued to write prolifically, producing some of her most acclaimed works in the years following the incident. Her novels, such as "The Murder of Roger Ackroyd," "Murder on the Orient Express," and "Death on the Nile," solidified her reputation as the "Queen of Crime" and ensured her place in literary history. The intrigue surrounding her disappearance added an extra layer of mystique to her persona and may have even contributed to the enduring fascination with her work.

The story of Agatha Christie's disappearance also highlights broader themes of gender, fame, and mental health. As a successful female author in the early 20th century, Christie faced unique pressures and expectations. Her disappearance and the subsequent public reaction underscore the challenges of managing personal struggles while living in the public eye. The case also draws attention to the stigmatization of mental health issues during that era and the limited understanding of conditions such as amnesia and depression.

In exploring the disappearance of Agatha Christie, it is essential to consider the social and cultural context of the 1920s. The post-World War I period was a time of significant change and upheaval, with shifts in societal norms and expectations. For a woman like Christie, navigating the complexities of fame, marital discord, and grief would have been particularly challenging. Her disappearance can be seen as a response to the overwhelming pressures she faced, reflecting a moment of crisis in her otherwise successful life.

The legacy of Agatha Christie's disappearance continues to be a topic of fascination and study. Biographers such as Janet Morgan and Laura Thompson have delved into the mystery, offering various interpretations based on available evidence and psychological insights. Fictionalized accounts, such as the novel "The Mystery of Mrs. Christie" by Marie Benedict and the film "Agatha" starring Vanessa Redgrave and Dustin Hoffman, have also explored different aspects of the case, blending fact and fiction to create compelling narratives.

Ultimately, the disappearance of Agatha Christie remains an enigmatic chapter in the life of one of the world's most beloved authors. While the true reasons behind her actions may never be fully understood, the incident adds a humanizing dimension to her story, reminding us that even those who create mysteries can find themselves entangled in real-life enigmas. Christie's ability to continue writing and producing masterpieces after such a profound personal crisis is a testament to her resilience and talent, further cementing her legacy as a literary icon.

As we reflect on the disappearance of Agatha Christie, we are reminded of the enduring allure of mystery and the complexities of the human mind. The unanswered questions surrounding her disappearance invite us to consider the interplay between fact and fiction, reality and perception, in our understanding of historical events. Christie's own words, characters, and plots continue to captivate readers around the world, ensuring that the mystery of her disappearance remains a topic of intrigue and speculation for generations to come.

Chapter 32: The Death of Heath Ledger

The death of Heath Ledger on January 22, 2008, at the age of 28, was a tragic and shocking event that resonated deeply within the entertainment industry and among his fans worldwide. Ledger, an Australian actor known for his compelling performances and versatility, had just delivered a career-defining portrayal of the Joker in Christopher Nolan's "The Dark Knight." His untimely passing left a void in Hollywood and led to widespread speculation and reflection on the pressures and challenges faced by those in the spotlight.

Heath Andrew Ledger was born on April 4, 1979, in Perth, Western Australia. From a young age, Ledger demonstrated a passion for acting and the arts, participating in school plays and community theater. His natural talent and charisma quickly set him apart, and he pursued a career in acting with determination. Ledger moved to Sydney at the age of 17, where he landed roles in Australian television series such as "Sweat" and "Home and Away." His breakthrough came with the film "Two Hands" in 1999, which showcased his potential as a leading man.

Ledger's Hollywood career took off when he was cast in the teen comedy "10 Things I Hate About You" (1999), a modern adaptation of Shakespeare's "The Taming of the Shrew." His performance as the charming and rebellious Patrick Verona made him a heartthrob and a rising star in the industry. He continued to build his reputation with roles in films such as "The Patriot" (2000), alongside Mel Gibson, and "A Knight's Tale" (2001), where he played the lead role of William Thatcher, a peasant who aspires to be a knight.

Despite his early success in romantic comedies and action-adventure films, Ledger sought to challenge himself with more complex and diverse roles. He deliberately chose projects that would push him as an actor and allow him to explore different facets of his craft. This approach led to critically acclaimed performances in films such as "Monster's Ball" (2001), where he played a troubled prison guard, and "Ned Kelly" (2003), in which he portrayed the infamous Australian outlaw.

Ledger's commitment to his craft was further exemplified by his portrayal of Ennis Del Mar in Ang Lee's "Brokeback Mountain" (2005). The film, which told the story of a forbidden and secretive relationship between two cowboys, was groundbreaking in its depiction of LGBTQ+ themes. Ledger's performance was widely praised for its depth and authenticity, earning him an Academy Award nomination for Best Actor. His nuanced portrayal of Ennis Del Mar solidified his reputation as a serious and talented actor capable of tackling emotionally challenging roles.

As Ledger's career progressed, he continued to seek out roles that allowed him to explore darker and more complex characters. This pursuit of artistic growth and authenticity ultimately led him to one of his most iconic roles: the Joker in Christopher Nolan's "The Dark Knight" (2008). Ledger's preparation for the role was intense and immersive. He isolated himself in a hotel room for weeks, developing the character's distinctive voice, mannerisms, and psychological profile. His portrayal of the Joker was both mesmerizing and terrifying, earning widespread acclaim and a posthumous Academy Award for Best Supporting Actor.

The immense dedication Ledger brought to his craft, particularly in his role as the Joker, took a toll on his mental and physical health. He described the experience as exhausting and admitted to having trouble sleeping during the filming process. In interviews, Ledger spoke candidly about the pressures and anxieties he faced as an actor, as well as his struggles with insomnia. He sought medical help and was prescribed a combination of medications, including sleeping pills and anti-anxiety drugs.

On January 22, 2008, Heath Ledger was found unresponsive in his Manhattan apartment by his housekeeper and masseuse. Despite their efforts to revive him, Ledger was pronounced dead at the scene. The initial shock and disbelief surrounding his death quickly gave way to questions about the cause. An autopsy was performed, and the New York City Medical Examiner's Office later determined that Ledger died as a result of acute intoxication from the combined effects of oxycodone, hydrocodone, diazepam, temazepam, alprazolam, and doxylamine. The death was ruled accidental, emphasizing the dangers of combining prescription medications without proper medical supervision.

Ledger's death prompted an outpouring of grief and tributes from fans, colleagues, and the broader entertainment industry. Fellow actors and directors praised his talent, work ethic, and the profound impact he had on those who worked with him. Christopher Nolan, the director of "The Dark Knight," described Ledger as "an extraordinary person, an extraordinary talent," and expressed his deep sorrow at the loss.

In the wake of Ledger's passing, there was significant media coverage and public discourse about the pressures faced by actors and the potential for substance abuse and mental health issues within the industry. The incident highlighted the need for greater awareness and support for mental health, as well as the importance of responsible prescription medication use. Ledger's death served as a tragic reminder of the challenges that can accompany fame and success, particularly for those who are deeply committed to their craft.

Ledger's family, including his parents and sisters, expressed their grief and appreciation for the support they received from the public. His former partner, actress Michelle Williams, with whom he had a daughter, Matilda, also mourned his loss. Williams spoke of Ledger's deep love for their daughter and the profound impact his death had on their lives.

In addition to his contributions to film, Ledger was also involved in various charitable endeavors. He supported organizations such as the

Australian-based "Heath Ledger Scholarship," which provides financial assistance and professional support to emerging Australian actors. This legacy of giving back to the acting community reflects Ledger's commitment to nurturing talent and his desire to make a positive impact beyond his own career.

Ledger's final film role was in Terry Gilliam's "The Imaginarium of Doctor Parnassus" (2009). At the time of his death, Ledger had completed some of the filming, but significant portions of the film remained unfinished. In a unique and heartfelt tribute, Gilliam enlisted the help of actors Johnny Depp, Jude Law, and Colin Farrell to complete Ledger's role. The film's narrative was adjusted to accommodate this change, with each actor playing a different incarnation of Ledger's character. This collaborative effort allowed the film to be completed and released, serving as a poignant reminder of Ledger's talent and the respect he commanded among his peers.

Heath Ledger's legacy continues to be celebrated through his body of work, which includes a diverse range of performances that showcase his versatility and dedication as an actor. Films such as "Brokeback Mountain," "The Dark Knight," and "A Knight's Tale" remain beloved by audiences and critics alike, serving as lasting testaments to his talent and artistry. Ledger's portrayal of the Joker, in particular, has become iconic, influencing subsequent portrayals of the character and earning a place in the pantheon of great cinematic performances.

In the years since Ledger's death, there have been numerous retrospectives, documentaries, and books dedicated to exploring his life and career. These works often highlight the depth of his commitment to his roles and the profound impact he had on those who knew him. They also emphasize the tragedy of his untimely passing and the potential for even greater achievements that were left unrealized.

One such documentary, "I Am Heath Ledger," released in 2017, provides an intimate look at Ledger's life through home videos, interviews with family and friends, and behind-the-scenes footage. The film offers a glimpse into Ledger's creative process, his passions, and his relationships, painting a portrait of a multifaceted individual who was deeply committed to his craft and loved by those who knew him.

Heath Ledger's influence on the acting community and popular culture is undeniable. His willingness to take risks and push the boundaries of his craft has inspired countless actors and filmmakers. Ledger's legacy is also evident in the ongoing discussions about mental health and the pressures faced by those in the entertainment industry. His death has served as a catalyst for increased awareness and support for mental health initiatives, helping to destigmatize issues such as anxiety, depression, and substance abuse.

In reflecting on the life and career of Heath Ledger, it is important to recognize the complexity of his journey. He was an immensely talented and dedicated actor who left an indelible mark on the world of film. His performances continue to resonate with audiences, and his legacy as an artist and individual endures. While his death was a profound loss, his contributions to cinema and his impact on those who knew him will be remembered for generations to come.

The death of Heath Ledger remains a poignant reminder of the fragility of life and the importance of mental health and support for those in high-pressure environments. It underscores the need for compassion, understanding, and awareness in addressing the challenges faced by individuals in the public eye. Ledger's story is one of talent, dedication, and a relentless pursuit of artistic excellence, and it continues to inspire and move people around the world.

Chapter 33: The Unsolved Murder of Chandra Levy

The unsolved murder of Chandra Levy is a case that has captivated the public and media since her disappearance in 2001. Chandra Ann Levy was a 24-year-old intern with the Federal Bureau of Prisons in Washington, D.C., and her sudden disappearance and subsequent death drew intense scrutiny, speculation, and a prolonged investigation that remains unresolved.

Chandra Levy was born on April 14, 1977, in Cleveland, Ohio, and grew up in Modesto, California. She graduated from San Francisco State University with a degree in journalism and was pursuing a master's degree in public administration from the University of Southern California (USC). As part of her studies, she secured an internship in Washington, D.C., with the Federal Bureau of Prisons. This opportunity placed her in the heart of the nation's capital, where she aspired to build a career in government service.

Levy's disappearance on May 1, 2001, set off alarm bells among her family and friends. She had been living in Washington, D.C., for her internship but was preparing to return to California. Her parents, Robert and Susan Levy, became concerned when they could not reach her and contacted the police. The subsequent investigation revealed that Levy had last been seen at her apartment and had emailed her landlord about vacating the premises. Her personal belongings, including her wallet, identification, and credit cards, were found in her apartment, but there was no sign of a struggle or foul play.

The case gained national attention when it was revealed that Levy had been romantically involved with Gary Condit, a married U.S. Congressman from California. Condit, who was in his early 50s at the time, initially denied any involvement with Levy but later admitted to the relationship under police questioning. This revelation fueled intense media speculation and placed Condit under public scrutiny. Despite the focus on Condit, there was no evidence directly linking him to Levy's disappearance, and he consistently denied any involvement in her disappearance or death.

As the investigation continued, the Metropolitan Police Department (MPD) faced criticism for their handling of the case. Early missteps, including a delayed search of Levy's apartment and a failure to secure crucial evidence, hindered the investigation. The case also highlighted the challenges of dealing with high-profile investigations in the age of 24-hour news cycles and intense media scrutiny.

On May 22, 2002, over a year after her disappearance, the skeletal remains of Chandra Levy were discovered by a man walking his dog in Rock Creek Park, a large urban park in Washington, D.C. The discovery was made in a secluded area, and the remains were identified through dental records. The location where Levy's remains were found was about four miles from her apartment, and her clothing and personal items were scattered nearby. The cause of death was determined to be homicide, but the exact circumstances of her death remained unclear due to the decomposition of the body.

Following the discovery of Levy's remains, the focus of the investigation shifted to finding her killer. The MPD, along with the FBI and other law enforcement agencies, conducted a thorough search of the area and re-examined the evidence. The case took a significant turn in 2008 when a new suspect emerged: Ingmar Guandique, a Salvadoran immigrant who was already serving a prison sentence for attacking two other women in Rock Creek Park around the time of Levy's disappearance.

Guandique's history of violent attacks in the same park where Levy's remains were found made him a person of interest. The two women who survived his attacks provided testimonies that painted a picture of Guandique as a dangerous predator. Based on this new information, the authorities charged Guandique with Levy's murder in

March 2009. The trial began in October 2010, and the prosecution's case relied heavily on circumstantial evidence, including the similarities between Levy's disappearance and the attacks on the other women, as well as statements made by Guandique to fellow inmates about his involvement in Levy's death.

In November 2010, Guandique was found guilty of first-degree murder and other related charges. He was sentenced to 60 years in prison in February 2011. The conviction brought some closure to Levy's family, who had endured years of uncertainty and anguish. However, the case was far from over. In the years that followed, questions about the integrity of the investigation and the reliability of the evidence against Guandique persisted.

In 2015, new developments cast doubt on Guandique's conviction. The defense presented evidence that one of the key witnesses, an inmate who had testified that Guandique had confessed to him, had credibility issues. Additionally, it was revealed that the prosecution had withheld information that could have impeached this witness's testimony. In light of these revelations, a judge granted Guandique a new trial.

In July 2016, the charges against Guandique were dropped, and he was released from prison. The decision was based on the lack of sufficient evidence to secure a conviction, as well as the issues surrounding the credibility of the key witness. This turn of events reignited public interest in the case and underscored the complexities and challenges of solving high-profile, long-standing murder cases.

The unsolved murder of Chandra Levy remains a source of frustration and heartache for her family and friends. The case has highlighted the difficulties faced by law enforcement in investigating cases that lack clear evidence and the impact of media scrutiny on the judicial process. Despite the extensive investigation and the temporary conviction of a suspect, the true circumstances of Levy's death are still unknown.

Several theories have emerged over the years regarding what might have happened to Chandra Levy. Some believe that her relationship with Gary Condit played a more significant role than was officially acknowledged, while others speculate that she may have been the victim of a random act of violence unrelated to her personal life. The presence of known predators like Ingmar Guandique in the area where her remains were found supports the possibility of an opportunistic attack. However, without conclusive evidence, these theories remain speculative.

The case has also sparked discussions about the safety of young interns and the vulnerabilities they may face while living and working in unfamiliar environments. Levy's death served as a stark reminder of the dangers that can exist even in seemingly safe settings, prompting calls for better support and protection for interns and other young professionals.

Chandra Levy's legacy endures through the efforts of her family and advocacy organizations dedicated to improving safety and security for young people in similar circumstances. The Chandra Levy Foundation, established by her parents, aims to prevent violence against young adults and provides resources and support for families of missing persons. The foundation's work continues to honor Chandra's memory and seeks to ensure that others do not suffer a similar fate.

The enduring mystery of Chandra Levy's murder remains a poignant and unsettling chapter in the annals of unsolved crimes. The case exemplifies the complexities and frustrations inherent in criminal investigations, particularly those involving high-profile individuals and media scrutiny. It serves as a reminder of the importance of thorough and meticulous investigative work, the need for transparency and accountability in the judicial process, and the ongoing quest for justice for victims and their families.

As the years pass, the hope for new evidence or breakthroughs in the case persists. Advances in forensic technology and investigative techniques may one day provide the answers that have eluded investigators for so long. Until then, the unsolved murder of Chandra Levy remains a haunting reminder of the fragility of life and the enduring quest for justice in the face of tragedy.

Chapter 34: The Mystery of the Hinterkaifeck Murders

The Hinterkaifeck murders, a chilling and enigmatic case, occurred in March 1922 on a small Bavarian farmstead located about 70 kilometers north of Munich, Germany. This unsolved crime, involving the brutal slayings of six people, continues to baffle investigators and enthusiasts alike, and the mystery surrounding it has only deepened over the decades. The victims were Andreas Gruber, 63, his wife Cäzilia, 72, their widowed daughter Viktoria Gabriel, 35, and Viktoria's children, Cäzilia, 7, and Josef, 2. The maid, Maria Baumgartner, 44, who had only started working at the farm the day before the murders, was also among the dead.

The Gruber family was not well-liked in the rural community. Andreas Gruber was known to be a harsh and abusive man, with rumors of an incestuous relationship with his daughter Viktoria circulating widely. Despite these rumors and the family's isolation, the farm was prosperous. Days before the murders, Andreas had noticed strange occurrences, such as footprints in the snow leading to the house but none leading away, sounds of footsteps in the attic, and a set of keys going missing. These ominous signs suggested that someone might have been lurking around the property, adding a layer of foreboding to the tragic events that would soon unfold.

On the evening of March 31, 1922, the Gruber family and their maid were brutally murdered with a mattock, a type of pickaxe commonly used for farming. The perpetrator or perpetrators used the mattock to bludgeon each victim to death, showing no mercy even to the children. Strangely, the bodies of Andreas, Cäzilia, Viktoria, and the young Cäzilia were found stacked on top of each other in the barn, covered with hay. Maria Baumgartner and little Josef were killed in their beds, suggesting they might have been asleep when they were attacked.

The discovery of the bodies was delayed until April 4, when neighbors, concerned by the family's uncharacteristic absence and the fact that young Cäzilia had missed school, decided to investigate. Upon entering the farm, they were met with the gruesome scene. Police were called to the site, and the initial investigation began. However, the crime scene was poorly handled, with numerous people tramping through the farm and disturbing potential evidence before law enforcement arrived.

During the investigation, several puzzling details came to light. Despite the horrific murders, the farm animals had been fed, and neighbors reported seeing smoke coming from the chimney over the weekend following the murders. This indicated that the killer or killers might have stayed at the farm for several days after committing the crimes, possibly even eating meals there. Additionally, the family's dog, which was usually aggressive toward strangers, was found tied up but unharmed, suggesting that the dog either knew the perpetrator or was subdued by them.

The police conducted numerous interviews and pursued several leads, but no definitive suspect emerged. Theories abounded, ranging from a crime of passion to a robbery gone wrong. One of the more sensational theories involved the possibility of Viktoria's husband, Karl Gabriel, who was believed to have been killed in World War I, having returned from the dead to commit the murders. However, there was no concrete evidence to support this, and it was generally dismissed.

Another suspect was Lorenz Schlittenbauer, a neighbor and the alleged father of Viktoria's son, Josef. Schlittenbauer had a contentious relationship with the Grubers, particularly with Andreas, and he was one of the first to discover the bodies. His behavior during the initial discovery was considered suspicious by some; he seemed remarkably calm and composed, and he reportedly untied the family dog, potentially contaminating the crime scene. Schlittenbauer's motive, if any, could have stemmed from personal grievances or financial disputes, but again, no solid evidence linked him to the crime.

In 1923, a year after the murders, the Hinterkaifeck farmstead was demolished, and during the demolition, the mattock believed to be the murder weapon was found hidden in the attic. Despite this discovery, the trail had gone cold, and the case remained unsolved. In subsequent years, the investigation would be revisited, but each time, it yielded no new breakthroughs.

The mystery of the Hinterkaifeck murders has continued to intrigue and haunt those who study it. Various theories have been proposed over the years, some more plausible than others. One theory suggests that a vagrant or drifter, possibly a deserter from the war, could have been responsible for the murders. The isolated location of the farm would have made it an easy target, and the killer's knowledge of the family's routines and the layout of the farm indicates that they had likely been spying on the Grubers for some time.

Another theory posits that the murders were the result of a deeply personal vendetta, possibly connected to the dark secrets within the Gruber family. The alleged incestuous relationship between Andreas and Viktoria and the question of Josef's paternity added a layer of complexity to the case. If the murders were motivated by personal grievances, the killer might have been someone who knew the family well and harbored intense hatred or jealousy.

Despite the numerous theories and suspects, the Hinterkaifeck murders remain officially unsolved. The passage of time and the loss of potential evidence have made it increasingly unlikely that the case will ever be conclusively solved. However, the mystery continues to captivate true crime enthusiasts and researchers, who analyze the available evidence and speculate on possible scenarios.

In modern times, the case has been the subject of numerous books, documentaries, and even podcasts, each attempting to shed light on the elusive truth behind the murders. Advances in forensic science, such as DNA analysis, have raised hopes that new techniques might eventually uncover clues that were previously inaccessible. However, given the degradation of evidence over nearly a century, such breakthroughs are considered improbable.

The Hinterkaifeck murders serve as a grim reminder of the capacity for human violence and the dark secrets that can fester within families and communities. The case's enduring mystery lies not only in the brutality of the crime but also in the enigmatic nature of the perpetrators, who, despite their close proximity to the victims and the time they spent at the farm, managed to evade detection and capture. The haunting images of the isolated farmhouse, the brutalized bodies, and the unanswered questions continue to resonate, making the Hinterkaifeck murders one of the most chilling and enduring unsolved mysteries in criminal history.

The impact of the Hinterkaifeck murders extends beyond the immediate horror of the crime. It highlights the limitations of early 20th-century forensic and investigative techniques, and the importance of proper crime scene management, which was sorely lacking in this case. The bungled investigation, with its mishandling of evidence and delayed responses, underscores the challenges law enforcement faced during that era. In many ways, the Hinterkaifeck murders catalyzed changes in investigative procedures and the importance of preserving crime scenes, lessons that have influenced modern criminal investigations.

As time marches on, the Hinterkaifeck murders remain an eerie puzzle, a dark chapter in the annals of unsolved crimes that continues to fascinate and disturb. The farmstead where the murders took place has long since been replaced, but the memory of the brutal slayings endures. For those who delve into the mystery, the Hinterkaifeck murders offer a stark glimpse into a bygone era, where isolation and secrets could lead to unimaginable violence, and justice, elusive and frail, could be forever denied.

Chapter 35: The Enigma of the Sodder Children

The enigma of the Sodder children is one of the most perplexing and enduring mysteries in American history. The case revolves around the disappearance of five children from the Sodder family home in Fayetteville, West Virginia, on Christmas Eve in 1945. Despite decades of investigation, the fate of the children remains unknown, shrouded in a combination of tragedy, conspiracy, and unanswered questions.

The Sodder family consisted of George and Jennie Sodder and their ten children: John, Joe, Marion, George Jr., Maurice, Martha, Louis, Jennie, Betty, and Sylvia. George was an Italian immigrant who had built a successful trucking business. The family was well-regarded in their community, but George was known for his strong opinions, especially his outspoken criticism of Italian dictator Benito Mussolini, which led to some tension with other members of the local Italian-American community.

On the night of December 24, 1945, the Sodder children hung up their stockings and prepared for Christmas. Jennie allowed some of the children to stay up late and play with new toys while she and George went to bed. Around 1:00 a.m., Jennie was awakened by the sound of a telephone ringing. She answered the call and spoke briefly with a woman whose voice she did not recognize, asking for someone who did not live in the house. After hanging up, Jennie noticed that the lights were still on and the curtains open, which was unusual, but she turned off the lights, closed the curtains, and went back to bed.

Shortly after, Jennie was awakened again by the sound of something hitting the roof and then rolling off. A few minutes later, she smelled smoke and discovered that the house was on fire. She woke George, and the couple frantically tried to save their children. They managed to get four of their children out of the house, but the staircase to the attic, where the remaining five children slept, was engulfed in flames, making it impossible to reach them.

George and Jennie attempted to call the fire department but found that the phone was dead. George ran to a neighbor's house to use their phone, but the operator did not respond. Another neighbor drove into town to alert the fire department, but due to it being Christmas Eve and the war, the local fire department was understaffed and slow to respond. The fire department, composed largely of volunteers, did not arrive at the scene until about 8:00 a.m., by which time the house had been reduced to ashes.

Initial investigations concluded that the fire was caused by faulty wiring, but the circumstances surrounding the fire and the disappearance of the five children—Maurice, 14; Martha, 12; Louis, 9; Jennie, 8; and Betty, 5—raised numerous questions and doubts. Despite the intense heat of the fire, no remains of the children were found in the ashes. Experts stated that bones and other remains should have been found, leading to speculation that the children had been kidnapped and the fire set to cover the crime.

Several strange occurrences and pieces of evidence seemed to support this theory. A telephone repairman found that the house's phone line had been cut, not burned. A man was seen stealing a block and tackle from the property around the time of the fire, and a woman claimed to have seen the missing children in a car as the fire was raging. Months later, a woman in a Charleston hotel said she saw four of the children with two men and two women of "Italian extraction," who appeared to be hostile and prevented her from talking to the children.

George Sodder conducted his own investigation, combing through the ruins and finding various artifacts, including a piece of an appliance that was not originally in the house. He also noted that a ladder that had been missing during the fire was found at the bottom of an embankment 75 feet away. Additionally, the family received a postcard from Kentucky with a photograph of a young man resembling their son

Louis, along with a cryptic note reading, "Louis Sodder. I love brother Frankie. Ilil Boys. A90132 or 35."

The Sodders remained convinced that their children had been abducted and continued to seek answers. They erected a billboard along Route 16, offering a $5,000 reward for information leading to the recovery of their children, later increasing it to $10,000. The billboard remained in place for decades and became a symbol of the family's enduring hope and determination to find out what happened.

Over the years, numerous theories and speculations have been proposed. Some believe the children were taken by individuals with ties to George's political views and conflicts within the Italian immigrant community. Others suggest that the Mafia might have been involved, possibly in retaliation for George's outspoken criticism of Mussolini. Another theory is that the children were taken by someone they knew and trusted, which would explain why they left the house without a struggle.

Despite the family's efforts and the attention brought to the case, no conclusive evidence has ever been found to explain what happened to the Sodder children. The case was reopened by the West Virginia State Police in 1968, but it led to no new findings. The mystery continues to captivate and baffle those who study it, with many questions remaining unanswered.

The enigma of the Sodder children is a poignant and haunting reminder of the pain and uncertainty that can accompany unsolved mysteries. George and Jennie Sodder never gave up hope of finding their children, and their relentless pursuit of the truth became a defining aspect of their lives. Jennie Sodder wore black in mourning for the rest of her life, and the family continued to follow up on leads and tips, no matter how tenuous, until the deaths of George in 1969 and Jennie in 1989.

In the decades since the fire, the case has taken on a life of its own, inspiring countless articles, books, and documentaries. It has become a part of local lore in Fayetteville and a subject of enduring fascination for true crime enthusiasts. The story of the Sodder family highlights the profound impact of loss and the lengths to which people will go to seek justice and closure for their loved ones.

The mystery of the Sodder children is not just a story of a tragic fire and missing children; it is also a tale of resilience, hope, and the unbreakable bonds of family. The Sodders' unwavering belief that their children might still be alive somewhere in the world, and their tireless efforts to find them, resonate deeply with anyone who has experienced the pain of losing a loved one under mysterious circumstances.

While the fate of the Sodder children may never be known, their story continues to remind us of the importance of persistence in the face of uncertainty and the enduring power of a family's love. The billboard that once stood along Route 16 may be gone, but the memory of the Sodder family's search for answers endures, a testament to the human spirit's capacity for hope and determination in the face of seemingly insurmountable odds.

Chapter 36: The Disappearance of Madeleine McCann

The disappearance of Madeleine McCann is one of the most infamous and heart-wrenching missing persons cases in modern history. Madeleine Beth McCann, a three-year-old British girl, vanished from her family's holiday apartment in Praia da Luz, a resort town in the Algarve region of Portugal, on the evening of May 3, 2007. The case has captivated the world, involving extensive media coverage, numerous investigations, and an array of theories, yet it remains unsolved.

Madeleine was born on May 12, 2003, in Leicester, England, to Kate and Gerry McCann. Both parents were respected medical professionals, with Kate working as a general practitioner and Gerry as a cardiologist. The family, including Madeleine and her younger twin siblings, Sean and Amelie, embarked on a week-long vacation to Portugal, staying at the Ocean Club Resort in Praia da Luz. They were joined by seven friends and their children, a group often referred to as the "Tapas Seven."

On the night of Madeleine's disappearance, her parents and their friends dined at a tapas restaurant located about 55 meters from the McCanns' ground-floor apartment, 5A. The adults had established a routine of checking on their sleeping children at regular intervals throughout the evening. At around 8:30 p.m., Kate and Gerry left their apartment, leaving the three children asleep. Gerry checked on them at approximately 9:05 p.m., finding everything in order. Jane Tanner, one of their friends, reported seeing a man carrying a child away from the direction of the McCanns' apartment around 9:15 p.m., but this sighting was not immediately linked to Madeleine's disappearance.

Kate went to check on the children at around 10:00 p.m. and discovered that Madeleine was missing. The window to the children's bedroom was open, and the shutters were raised. In a state of panic,

Kate ran back to the restaurant, shouting, "Madeleine's gone! Someone's taken her!" The ensuing hours saw frantic searches by resort staff and local police, but no trace of Madeleine was found.

The initial investigation by the Portuguese police, the Polícia Judiciária (PJ), was heavily criticized for its handling. Key procedural errors, such as not securing the crime scene and failing to notify border authorities immediately, likely compromised potential evidence. As days turned into weeks, the case garnered massive media attention worldwide, with Madeleine's distinctive right eye, featuring a coloboma of the iris, making her instantly recognizable.

The PJ initially worked on the assumption that Madeleine had been abducted. However, as the investigation progressed, suspicions began to form around Kate and Gerry McCann. On September 7, 2007, they were named as formal suspects, or "arguidos," in the case. This development was based on circumstantial evidence, including the detection of cadaver dogs and forensic analyses that were later contested for their accuracy. The McCanns vehemently denied any involvement in their daughter's disappearance and were eventually cleared of suspect status in July 2008.

During this period, numerous theories emerged. Some posited that Madeleine had been abducted by a pedophile ring, while others suggested she had been sold into human trafficking. The sighting reported by Jane Tanner fueled the theory of an abduction, with the suspect becoming known as "Tanner Man." Later, a sighting by another British tourist, Martin Smith, suggested a man carrying a child toward the beach, and this individual became known as "Smith Man." These conflicting descriptions added to the complexity of the investigation.

In 2011, under significant public pressure and media scrutiny, Scotland Yard launched its own investigation, Operation Grange, led by Detective Chief Inspector Andy Redwood. The review, which began in May 2011, aimed to reassess all available evidence and pursue new leads. Operation Grange released an age-progressed image of

Madeleine and refocused the investigation on the possibility of an abduction.

In 2013, Operation Grange identified several persons of interest and publicly appealed for information about these individuals. They also released e-fits of potential suspects, including "Smith Man," whose sighting was considered highly significant. Despite these efforts, no conclusive breakthroughs were made, and the search for Madeleine continued.

In addition to law enforcement efforts, the McCanns hired private investigators to explore leads and potential sightings. Over the years, there have been numerous reported sightings of Madeleine from various countries, including Spain, Morocco, and even Australia, but none have been substantiated.

In June 2020, a significant development occurred when German authorities announced that they had identified a new suspect in the case, a 43-year-old German man named Christian Brückner. Brückner, a convicted sex offender with a history of crimes against children, was living in the Algarve region at the time of Madeleine's disappearance. He had previously been convicted of raping a 72-year-old American woman in Praia da Luz in 2005, near the McCanns' holiday apartment.

The German authorities, led by prosecutor Hans Christian Wolters, stated they had evidence suggesting that Madeleine was dead and believed Brückner was responsible for her abduction and murder. They appealed to the public for more information about Brückner's activities around the time of Madeleine's disappearance. Despite this announcement, the evidence against Brückner has not been disclosed in detail, and no charges have been filed.

The disappearance of Madeleine McCann has had profound and lasting impacts on her family, the community, and the wider public. For Kate and Gerry McCann, the ordeal has been a relentless quest for answers, marked by extensive media coverage, public scrutiny, and legal battles. They established the Madeleine McCann Fund to finance the search for their daughter and to support families of missing children. The fund has been instrumental in keeping the case in the public eye and financing private investigations.

The case has also prompted discussions about the responsibilities and challenges faced by parents traveling with young children. The McCanns faced considerable criticism for leaving their children unattended, even though they were within sight of the restaurant. This aspect of the case has been debated extensively, highlighting the difficulties and judgments parents can face in balancing vigilance and trust.

Furthermore, the case has spurred changes in the way missing children cases are handled internationally. It underscored the importance of rapid and coordinated responses from law enforcement, media engagement, and public awareness. The extensive media coverage of Madeleine's disappearance, while sometimes intrusive, played a crucial role in mobilizing public interest and support.

Despite the ongoing investigations and numerous leads, the fate of Madeleine McCann remains one of the greatest unsolved mysteries of our time. The case exemplifies the complexities and challenges inherent in missing persons investigations, particularly those involving young children and international jurisdictions. It also highlights the enduring hope and determination of families to seek justice and answers, no matter how long the search may take.

As the years pass, the disappearance of Madeleine McCann continues to captivate and perplex, with new developments and theories emerging periodically. The case remains open, with law enforcement agencies in the UK, Portugal, and Germany maintaining active interest. For those who follow the story, the hope that Madeleine may still be found, or that new evidence may finally unravel the mystery, persists as a testament to the enduring human spirit and the quest for truth in the face of uncertainty.

Chapter 37: The Mysterious Death of Anna Nicole Smith

The mysterious death of Anna Nicole Smith is a story marked by glamour, controversy, and tragedy, mirroring the tumultuous life she led. Born Vickie Lynn Hogan on November 28, 1967, in Houston, Texas, Anna Nicole Smith rose from humble beginnings to become a famous model, actress, and television personality. Her life, filled with dramatic ups and downs, ended abruptly on February 8, 2007, in a Florida hotel room, leading to widespread speculation and intrigue.

Smith's early life was far from glamorous. She was raised primarily by her mother and aunt in the small town of Mexia, Texas, after her parents divorced when she was young. Dropping out of high school in the tenth grade, she married Billy Wayne Smith in 1985, with whom she had her first son, Daniel, in 1986. The marriage was short-lived, and Smith soon found herself working various low-paying jobs to support herself and her son.

In the late 1980s, Smith moved to Houston, where she started working at a strip club. It was there that she met several influential people who would help her break into the modeling world. Her big break came in 1992 when she sent photos to Playboy magazine, leading to her selection as Playboy Playmate of the Month in May 1992 and Playmate of the Year in 1993. This exposure catapulted her to fame, and she adopted the stage name Anna Nicole Smith, inspired by screen legend Marilyn Monroe, whom she idolized.

Smith's sudden rise to fame was marked by her striking looks and voluptuous figure, which led to lucrative modeling contracts, including a high-profile campaign with Guess jeans. Her appearance in these campaigns cemented her status as a pop culture icon of the 1990s, often drawing comparisons to Monroe. However, her life was also characterized by a series of personal and legal battles that would overshadow her professional success.

One of the most controversial aspects of Smith's life was her marriage to J. Howard Marshall II, an 89-year-old oil tycoon, in 1994. The 63-year age difference between the couple sparked widespread media attention and speculation about Smith's motivations. Critics accused her of marrying Marshall for his wealth, a claim she consistently denied, insisting that their relationship was based on love and mutual affection. Marshall died just 13 months after their marriage, triggering a protracted and highly publicized legal battle over his estate.

Smith's fight for Marshall's fortune pitted her against Marshall's son, E. Pierce Marshall, in a legal dispute that spanned more than a decade. Smith initially won a substantial settlement, but the ruling was overturned multiple times, culminating in a landmark case that reached the U.S. Supreme Court. In 2006, the Supreme Court ruled in Smith's favor, allowing her to pursue her claim in federal court, but the ultimate outcome remained unresolved at the time of her death.

Amidst her legal battles, Smith's personal life was also marked by turmoil. She struggled with substance abuse, which was widely documented in the media, and her erratic behavior often made headlines. Her reality television show, "The Anna Nicole Show," aired from 2002 to 2004, showcased her eccentric lifestyle and provided viewers with an intimate, albeit chaotic, glimpse into her life. While the show was popular, it also attracted criticism for exploiting Smith's vulnerabilities for entertainment.

Tragedy struck Smith in September 2006, when her 20-year-old son, Daniel, died suddenly in her hospital room in the Bahamas, just days after she gave birth to her daughter, Dannielynn. Daniel's death was later attributed to a combination of methadone and antidepressants, and it devastated Smith, who was reportedly inconsolable. The loss of her son marked the beginning of a downward spiral for Smith, who was already grappling with the pressures of fame, legal issues, and substance abuse.

Smith's own death on February 8, 2007, added another layer of mystery and speculation to her already controversial life. She was found unresponsive in her room at the Seminole Hard Rock Hotel and Casino in Hollywood, Florida. Despite attempts to revive her, Smith was pronounced dead at the scene. She was 39 years old. Her sudden death triggered an immediate media frenzy, with widespread speculation about the cause.

The official cause of Smith's death was later determined to be an accidental overdose of prescription drugs. The medical examiner's report listed the primary cause as "combined drug intoxication," with several medications found in her system, including chloral hydrate, a sedative; methadone, an opioid; and various anti-anxiety and anti-depressant medications. The report noted that Smith had been suffering from a variety of ailments, including chronic pain, anxiety, and depression, which likely contributed to her reliance on prescription drugs.

The circumstances surrounding Smith's death and the role of those around her led to numerous conspiracy theories and allegations. Howard K. Stern, Smith's lawyer and long-time companion, was present at the hotel when she died and became a central figure in the ensuing investigations. Stern, along with two doctors, was later charged with conspiracy to prescribe controlled substances to an addict, though all charges against Stern were eventually dismissed.

Smith's death also sparked a highly publicized paternity battle over her infant daughter, Dannielynn. Several men claimed to be the child's father, including Howard K. Stern and Larry Birkhead, a photographer with whom Smith had a brief relationship. After months of legal wrangling and DNA testing, Birkhead was confirmed as Dannielynn's biological father in April 2007. The paternity case attracted significant media attention, further complicating the already sensational narrative of Smith's life and death.

In the wake of her death, Smith's estate faced ongoing legal battles, including the unresolved dispute over J. Howard Marshall's fortune. In 2011, the U.S. Supreme Court ruled against Smith's estate, effectively ending the lengthy legal saga that had defined much of her adult life. Despite this, Smith's legacy continued to be a subject of fascination and debate, emblematic of the pitfalls and excesses of celebrity culture.

The mysterious death of Anna Nicole Smith is a tragic story that underscores the complexities and contradictions of her life. From her meteoric rise to fame as a Playboy model and Guess jeans spokeswoman to her tumultuous personal life and legal battles, Smith's journey was marked by both triumph and tragedy. Her untimely death, fueled by prescription drug use and compounded by personal loss and legal pressures, remains a poignant reminder of the vulnerabilities faced by those in the public eye.

Smith's life and death continue to captivate the public imagination, with numerous books, documentaries, and films exploring her story. Her legacy is a cautionary tale about the dark side of fame and the relentless scrutiny faced by celebrities. Despite the controversies and challenges she faced, Smith's enduring image as a glamorous, larger-than-life figure remains etched in popular culture.

In reflecting on Anna Nicole Smith's life, it is important to acknowledge both her humanity and the broader societal forces that shaped her story. Her struggles with substance abuse, mental health issues, and the pressures of fame are reflective of the challenges faced by many in the entertainment industry. Smith's story serves as a reminder of the importance of compassion, understanding, and support for those grappling with similar issues.

Ultimately, the mysterious death of Anna Nicole Smith is a story of a woman who, despite her flaws and missteps, sought love, validation, and success in a world that often seemed intent on exploiting her vulnerabilities. Her life, marked by both extraordinary highs and devastating lows, is a testament to the complexities of the human experience and the enduring allure of celebrity.

Chapter 38: The Unsolved Murder of Biggie Smalls

The unsolved murder of Christopher Wallace, better known by his stage names "The Notorious B.I.G." or "Biggie Smalls," remains one of the most perplexing mysteries in the history of modern music and criminal investigations. Born in Brooklyn, New York, in 1972, Wallace rose to fame in the early 1990s, becoming one of the most influential and iconic figures in hip-hop. His life and career were tragically cut short on March 9, 1997, when he was gunned down in Los Angeles at the age of 24.

On the night of his murder, Biggie had attended a party hosted by Vibe magazine and Qwest Records at the Petersen Automotive Museum in Los Angeles. The event was a celebration of his life and career, but it also marked the culmination of a tense and turbulent period in the hip-hop world. Just six months earlier, fellow rapper Tupac Shakur had been killed in a drive-by shooting in Las Vegas, and the rivalry between East Coast and West Coast rap factions was at a boiling point. The tension was palpable, and many believed that Biggie's life was in danger.

As the party ended, Biggie and his entourage left the museum and entered a GMC Suburban to head back to his hotel. At approximately 12:45 a.m., while stopped at a red light on the corner of Wilshire Boulevard and South Fairfax Avenue, a dark-colored Chevrolet Impala SS pulled up alongside the SUV. The driver of the Impala rolled down his window and fired multiple shots at Biggie, striking him four times. Despite being rushed to Cedars-Sinai Medical Center, Wallace was pronounced dead at 1:15 a.m. The murder sent shockwaves through the music community and beyond, leading to widespread mourning and an outpouring of grief from fans and fellow artists.

The investigation into Biggie's murder was plagued by numerous challenges and controversies from the outset. The Los Angeles Police Department (LAPD) faced intense scrutiny and criticism for its handling of the case. Conspiracy theories abounded, with many believing that corrupt police officers and gang affiliations played a role in the murder. Some speculated that Biggie's death was a retaliatory act in the ongoing East Coast-West Coast feud, while others suggested that it was linked to his connections with the Crips gang.

One of the most significant developments in the case came in 2002, when retired LAPD detective Russell Poole publicly accused fellow officers of being involved in the murder. Poole's investigation led him to believe that officers David Mack and Rafael Perez were complicit in the crime and had connections to Death Row Records, the label founded by Suge Knight. Poole's allegations gained traction and led to a civil lawsuit filed by Biggie's mother, Voletta Wallace, against the LAPD, alleging a cover-up and conspiracy. The lawsuit was eventually dismissed, but it fueled public distrust in the police and added to the cloud of mystery surrounding the case.

Despite numerous leads, theories, and extensive media coverage, the murder of Biggie Smalls remains unsolved to this day. Over the years, several books, documentaries, and investigative reports have attempted to shed light on the case, each presenting different theories and potential suspects. Some investigators have pointed to a man named Amir Muhammad, also known as Harry Billups, as a possible shooter, while others have suggested that Suge Knight orchestrated the hit from prison. The lack of concrete evidence and witness cooperation has hindered the investigation, leaving many questions unanswered.

In addition to the criminal investigation, Biggie's murder has had a lasting impact on the music industry and popular culture. His death, along with Tupac Shakur's, marked a turning point in hip-hop, prompting artists and fans to reflect on the violence and rivalry that had characterized the genre in the 1990s. Biggie's music, characterized by his deep voice, lyrical prowess, and storytelling ability, continues to influence and inspire new generations of artists. His posthumous albums, "Life After Death" and "Born Again," have cemented his legacy as one of the greatest rappers of all time.

The unsolved nature of Biggie's murder has also contributed to his mythos, transforming him into a symbol of the tragic and untimely loss of a brilliant talent. His life and death have been the subject of numerous artistic works, including the 2009 biographical film "Notorious," which dramatizes his rise to fame and the events leading up to his murder. The ongoing fascination with Biggie's story reflects a broader cultural obsession with mysteries, conspiracies, and the search for truth.

As the years pass, the hope of solving the case diminishes, but the desire for justice and closure for Biggie's family and fans remains strong. The unresolved nature of the murder serves as a reminder of the complexities and challenges inherent in high-profile criminal investigations. It also underscores the broader issues of systemic corruption, gang violence, and the impact of fame and fortune on individuals and communities.

Chapter 39: The Death of Cleopatra

The death of Cleopatra VII, the last active ruler of the Ptolemaic Kingdom of Egypt, is one of the most famous and enduring mysteries of the ancient world. Cleopatra's life and death have been the subject of fascination and speculation for centuries, immortalized in literature, art, and popular culture. Her demise marked the end of an era for both Egypt and the Hellenistic world, and it played a crucial role in the rise of the Roman Empire. The circumstances surrounding her death, however, remain shrouded in ambiguity and controversy.

Cleopatra was born in 69 BCE in Alexandria, a city founded by Alexander the Great and a hub of culture and learning in the ancient world. As a member of the Ptolemaic dynasty, she was a descendant of Ptolemy I Soter, one of Alexander's generals. Her early life was marked by political intrigue and familial conflict, as the Ptolemies were known for their internal strife and complex relationships. Cleopatra became co-ruler of Egypt with her younger brother Ptolemy XIII following the death of their father, Ptolemy XII, in 51 BCE. Their reign was fraught with tension, and Cleopatra soon found herself embroiled in a civil war against her brother.

Cleopatra's fortunes changed dramatically with the arrival of Julius Caesar in 48 BCE. The Roman general and statesman intervened in the Ptolemaic civil war, and Cleopatra famously had herself smuggled into Caesar's presence, wrapped in a carpet. Their ensuing relationship was both political and romantic, and Caesar's support helped Cleopatra secure her position as the sole ruler of Egypt. She bore him a son, Ptolemy XV Philopator Philometor Caesar, commonly known as Caesarion. However, Caesar's assassination in 44 BCE left Cleopatra in a precarious position once again.

The power vacuum in Rome following Caesar's death led to a new phase of civil war, with Cleopatra aligning herself with Mark Antony, one of Caesar's former allies and a member of the Second Triumvirate.

Their alliance was both strategic and passionate, resulting in a powerful political and romantic partnership. Antony and Cleopatra had three children together, and they sought to consolidate their power in the Eastern Mediterranean. Their relationship, however, put them at odds with Octavian, Caesar's adopted son and another member of the Triumvirate.

The conflict between Antony and Cleopatra on one side and Octavian on the other culminated in the naval Battle of Actium in 31 BCE. Antony and Cleopatra's forces were decisively defeated by Octavian's fleet, led by Agrippa. Following their defeat, Antony and Cleopatra fled to Egypt, where their situation became increasingly desperate. With Octavian's forces closing in on Alexandria, Antony, believing Cleopatra had already taken her own life, fell on his sword and died in her arms.

Cleopatra's death occurred shortly thereafter, in August of 30 BCE, and it has been the subject of much debate and speculation ever since. According to the most widely accepted account, Cleopatra committed suicide to avoid the humiliation of being paraded as a captive in Octavian's triumph in Rome. Ancient sources, including Plutarch and Suetonius, describe how she arranged for a venomous asp, a symbol of divine royalty, to be smuggled into her quarters. The asp supposedly bit her, leading to her death. This dramatic account has captivated imaginations for centuries, inspiring countless works of art, literature, and drama, including Shakespeare's famous play, "Antony and Cleopatra."

However, the historical accuracy of the asp narrative has been questioned by modern scholars. The logistics of smuggling a live snake into Cleopatra's heavily guarded quarters, as well as the practicalities of using an asp for suicide, have raised doubts. Some historians propose alternative methods of suicide, such as the use of poison. Cleopatra was known to have a keen interest in pharmacology and could have had access to various toxins. Plutarch himself mentions another version of the story, suggesting that Cleopatra used a poisonous ointment or a needle (possibly coated with poison) to take her own life.

The possibility of murder has also been considered. Some historians speculate that Octavian may have orchestrated Cleopatra's death to eliminate a potential rival and secure his control over Egypt. Cleopatra's intelligence, political acumen, and ability to rally support could have posed a threat to Octavian's ambitions. If Cleopatra had been captured and taken to Rome, she might have found a way to undermine Octavian's authority. While this theory is intriguing, there is no definitive evidence to support the idea that Cleopatra was murdered.

The aftermath of Cleopatra's death had profound implications for Egypt and the wider Mediterranean world. With her passing, Egypt became a province of the Roman Empire, ending centuries of Ptolemaic rule. Octavian, now known as Augustus, went on to consolidate his power and establish the Roman Empire, becoming its first emperor. The wealth and resources of Egypt bolstered Rome's economy and contributed to Augustus's efforts to stabilize and expand the empire.

Cleopatra's legacy has endured through the ages, not only as a historical figure but also as a symbol of political intrigue, romantic passion, and tragic destiny. Her life and death have been interpreted and reinterpreted in various cultural contexts, reflecting contemporary concerns and values. In the Renaissance, she was often depicted as a femme fatale, embodying both seduction and danger. In the 20th century, cinematic portrayals, such as Elizabeth Taylor's iconic performance in the 1963 film "Cleopatra," emphasized her beauty, charisma, and tragic love affair with Antony.

Modern scholarship continues to explore Cleopatra's multifaceted legacy, examining her role as a ruler, her diplomatic and military strategies, and her cultural impact. Recent archaeological discoveries and reassessments of historical sources have shed new light on her reign and the complexities of her relationship with Rome. Cleopatra remains a subject of fascination for historians, archaeologists, and the general public, embodying the enduring allure of ancient Egypt and the timeless appeal of a powerful, enigmatic woman.

Chapter 40: The Mysterious Demise of Karen Silkwood

Karen Silkwood was a chemical technician and union activist employed by the Kerr-McGee Cimarron Fuel Fabrication Site in Crescent, Oklahoma. Her mysterious and controversial death on November 13, 1974, remains one of the most debated and intriguing cases in American history. Silkwood's involvement in uncovering safety violations and potential corporate misconduct at the Kerr-McGee plant, combined with the circumstances surrounding her untimely demise, have sparked numerous investigations, lawsuits, and media portrayals, keeping her story in the public eye for decades.

Born on February 19, 1946, in Longview, Texas, Karen Gay Silkwood grew up in a working-class family and later moved to Oklahoma, where she married and had three children. Following her divorce, Silkwood began working at the Kerr-McGee plant, where she was assigned to inspect fuel rods for nuclear reactors. The plant produced plutonium pellets for nuclear reactors, and Silkwood's job involved handling radioactive materials, putting her at significant risk of exposure. Concerns about health and safety violations at the plant, combined with her growing awareness of the potential dangers of radiation, led Silkwood to become active in the Oil, Chemical, and Atomic Workers Union (OCAW).

Silkwood's dedication to union activities and her increasing unease about safety standards at the Kerr-McGee plant led her to take a prominent role in the union's efforts to address these issues. She was elected to the union's bargaining committee and was tasked with investigating health and safety violations at the plant. Silkwood began meticulously documenting incidents of contamination, inadequate safety measures, and potential falsification of inspection records. Her findings raised serious concerns about the plant's operations and the potential risks to workers and the surrounding community.

In the months leading up to her death, Silkwood reported several incidents of plutonium contamination, including instances where she herself tested positive for significant levels of radiation. On November 5, 1974, Silkwood discovered that her apartment and car were contaminated with plutonium. This raised suspicions about potential sabotage, as the levels of contamination were too high to have occurred accidentally. Silkwood's colleagues and supporters believed that she was being targeted for her whistleblowing activities and that her life was in danger.

On the evening of November 13, 1974, Karen Silkwood left a union meeting in Crescent, Oklahoma, to meet with a New York Times reporter and a union official in Oklahoma City. She was carrying a folder of documents that purportedly contained evidence of safety violations and misconduct at the Kerr-McGee plant. Silkwood never made it to the meeting. Her car, a white Honda Civic, was found wrecked on the side of State Highway 74, about 30 miles from her destination. Silkwood was dead, and the folder of documents she had been carrying was missing.

The initial investigation into Silkwood's death concluded that she had fallen asleep at the wheel, causing her car to veer off the road and crash. However, this explanation was met with skepticism from her family, friends, and union colleagues, who believed that she had been intentionally forced off the road or otherwise incapacitated. The lack of skid marks and the presence of dents and other damage to the rear of her car suggested the possibility of foul play. Additionally, toxicology reports indicated the presence of a sedative, methaqualone, in her system, raising further questions about the circumstances leading to the crash.

The mysterious nature of Silkwood's death prompted multiple investigations and legal actions. Her family filed a lawsuit against

Kerr-McGee, alleging that the company's negligence had led to her plutonium contamination and subsequent death. The trial, which began in 1979, brought to light numerous safety violations at the Kerr-McGee plant and revealed the company's efforts to downplay the risks associated with plutonium exposure. The jury ultimately awarded the Silkwood family $10.5 million in damages, although the verdict was later reduced on appeal and settled out of court for $1.38 million. Despite the settlement, the case underscored the serious health and safety concerns in the nuclear industry and highlighted the potential consequences for whistleblowers.

Silkwood's story received widespread media attention, inspiring books, documentaries, and the 1983 film "Silkwood," starring Meryl Streep as Karen Silkwood. The film dramatized her life, her activism, and the events leading up to her death, bringing her story to a broader audience and cementing her legacy as a symbol of the fight for workplace safety and corporate accountability. The film's portrayal of Silkwood's struggles and the unresolved questions surrounding her death contributed to the ongoing debate about the treatment of whistleblowers and the responsibilities of corporations in ensuring the safety and well-being of their employees.

The lingering doubts about the true cause of Silkwood's death have fueled numerous conspiracy theories and speculations. Some believe that she was deliberately silenced to prevent her from exposing the dangerous practices at the Kerr-McGee plant. Others suggest that she may have been the victim of a more extensive cover-up involving higher levels of government or industry officials. The lack of definitive answers and the conflicting accounts of the events leading up to her death have made it difficult to reach a consensus on what really happened to Karen Silkwood.

In the years following her death, Silkwood's case has had a lasting impact on the nuclear industry and the protection of whistleblowers. Her courageous actions in documenting and exposing safety violations at the Kerr-McGee plant led to increased scrutiny of nuclear facilities and greater awareness of the risks associated with plutonium exposure. The case also highlighted the need for stronger protections for employees who raise concerns about workplace safety and corporate misconduct. Legislation and regulatory changes inspired by Silkwood's story have sought to improve the oversight of nuclear facilities and ensure that workers can report safety violations without fear of retaliation.

Karen Silkwood's legacy continues to resonate today, serving as a powerful reminder of the importance of vigilance, accountability, and the protection of those who speak out against injustice. Her story is a testament to the potential impact of individual actions in challenging powerful institutions and advocating for the safety and well-being of workers. The unresolved questions surrounding her death keep her memory alive in the public consciousness, prompting ongoing reflection on the challenges faced by whistleblowers and the responsibilities of corporations to their employees and the broader community.

Chapter 41: The Disappearance of Harold Holt

The disappearance of Harold Holt, the 17th Prime Minister of Australia, is one of the most intriguing and enduring mysteries in Australian history. On December 17, 1967, Holt vanished while swimming in rough surf at Cheviot Beach near Portsea, Victoria, leading to a massive search and a flurry of speculation and conspiracy theories that have persisted for decades. His sudden disappearance not only shocked the nation but also left a legacy of unanswered questions and wild theories about what might have happened to the then-sitting Prime Minister.

Harold Edward Holt was born on August 5, 1908, in Sydney, New South Wales. He embarked on a career in law before entering politics, joining the United Australia Party (UAP) and later the Liberal Party of Australia. Holt quickly rose through the political ranks, known for his charismatic personality, eloquence, and dedication to public service. He held several ministerial positions before becoming the leader of the Liberal Party and the Prime Minister of Australia in January 1966, succeeding Sir Robert Menzies. As Prime Minister, Holt was a staunch ally of the United States, supporting Australia's involvement in the Vietnam War and fostering close ties with President Lyndon B. Johnson. His "All the way with LBJ" slogan became a hallmark of his tenure, reflecting his commitment to the ANZUS alliance.

On that fateful day in December 1967, Holt was spending the weekend at his beach house in Portsea. Despite the overcast weather and warnings about the dangerous conditions, he decided to go for a swim at Cheviot Beach, a spot known for its strong currents and unpredictable tides. Accompanied by several friends, including his rumored lover, Marjorie Gillespie, and her daughter, Holt entered the water and began swimming. Witnesses later recounted that Holt swam further out than usual, seemingly undeterred by the increasingly rough conditions. Moments later, he was seen struggling against the powerful waves before disappearing from sight.

The immediate response to Holt's disappearance was one of shock and disbelief. A massive search operation was launched, involving the Australian Navy, Air Force, Army, police, and numerous volunteers. Divers, helicopters, and boats scoured the area for any sign of Holt, but despite their extensive efforts, no trace of him was ever found. The official conclusion was that Holt had drowned, swept away by the treacherous currents. However, the lack of a body and the mysterious circumstances surrounding his disappearance fueled rampant speculation and a host of conspiracy theories.

One of the most popular theories suggested that Holt had faked his own death to escape the pressures of political life or to be with his alleged lover, Marjorie Gillespie. Proponents of this theory pointed to Holt's known love of adventure and his reputed dissatisfaction with the demands of being Prime Minister. However, those who knew Holt personally rejected this idea, citing his strong sense of duty and commitment to his role. Additionally, there was no concrete evidence to support the claim that Holt had staged his own disappearance.

Another theory posited that Holt had been assassinated, possibly by foreign agents or political enemies. Given the Cold War context and Holt's pro-American stance, some speculated that he had been targeted by communist spies or other hostile forces. One particularly outlandish version of this theory suggested that Holt had been abducted by a Chinese submarine. This idea gained some traction due to Holt's involvement in secretive international negotiations, but it was widely dismissed as implausible. The notion of a Chinese submarine operating undetected in Australian waters and abducting the Prime Minister was deemed far-fetched, lacking credible evidence.

A more mundane but plausible explanation is that Holt, an experienced swimmer who often underestimated the dangers of the ocean, simply misjudged the conditions that day. Cheviot Beach is known for its powerful undertows and unpredictable surf, and even strong swimmers can quickly find themselves in trouble. It is entirely possible that Holt, caught in a strong current or a rip, was unable to make it back to shore and drowned. This theory aligns with the official conclusion and the testimonies of those who witnessed the events, although the absence of a body still leaves room for doubt.

Holt's disappearance also prompted discussions about the safety and security protocols for high-ranking officials. At the time, there were no formal security arrangements in place for the Prime Minister during private outings. Holt's decision to swim in dangerous waters without adequate precautions highlighted the need for better protection and led to changes in how future Prime Ministers' safety was managed.

In the wake of Holt's disappearance, Australia faced a period of political uncertainty. Deputy Prime Minister John McEwen was sworn in as the acting Prime Minister, and a few weeks later, John Gorton was elected as the new leader of the Liberal Party and the 19th Prime Minister of Australia. Holt's sudden and mysterious disappearance cast a long shadow over his successor's tenure and remains a poignant chapter in Australian political history.

Over the years, Holt's legacy has been revisited through various forms of media, including books, documentaries, and even a 1985 television movie titled "The Prime Minister is Missing." These portrayals have kept the mystery alive in the public imagination, often focusing on the more sensational aspects of the case. Despite the passage of time, the enigma of what happened to Harold Holt endures, a tantalizing blend of fact, speculation, and myth.

In the broader context of Australian history, Holt's disappearance underscores the unpredictable nature of political life and the personal risks faced by public figures. It also serves as a reminder of the relentless power of nature, capable of overpowering even the most confident and experienced individuals. The case continues to fascinate and perplex, with each new generation encountering the story through different lenses and interpretations.

Chapter 42: The Unexplained Death of Princess Anastasia

The unexplained death of Princess Anastasia Romanov, the youngest daughter of Tsar Nicholas II of Russia, has captivated the world for over a century. Her mysterious fate, entangled with the broader tragedy of the Russian Revolution and the fall of the Romanov dynasty, has inspired countless books, films, and even animated features. The story of Anastasia's potential survival and the subsequent claims of various impostors have fueled enduring intrigue and speculation. This historical enigma is a complex tapestry of political upheaval, familial loyalty, and human resilience.

Anastasia Nikolaevna Romanov was born on June 18, 1901, into the illustrious Romanov dynasty, which had ruled Russia for over three centuries. She was the fourth daughter of Tsar Nicholas II and Tsarina Alexandra Feodorovna. Anastasia's childhood was marked by privilege and luxury, but also by the growing instability of the Russian Empire. Despite the grandeur of their surroundings, the Romanovs were known for their relatively simple lifestyle and close-knit family bonds. Anastasia, often described as a spirited and mischievous child, was particularly close to her siblings, especially her older sister, Maria.

The political landscape in Russia began to shift dramatically in the early 20th century. The Russo-Japanese War (1904-1905) and the subsequent Revolution of 1905 exposed deep-seated discontent within Russian society. The situation worsened during World War I, as Russia suffered severe military defeats and economic hardships. Tsar Nicholas II's decision to take direct command of the Russian army in 1915 further alienated him from the populace, leaving domestic governance to the Tsarina and the controversial mystic, Grigori Rasputin. Rasputin's influence over the royal family, particularly due to his perceived ability to heal the hemophilia of Anastasia's younger brother, Alexei, fueled public outrage and suspicion.

By 1917, Russia was on the brink of collapse. The February Revolution forced Nicholas II to abdicate the throne, ending over 300 years of Romanov rule. The former royal family was placed under house arrest, initially in the Alexander Palace at Tsarskoye Selo and later in Tobolsk, Siberia. In the fall of 1917, the Bolsheviks seized power in the October Revolution, and the Romanovs' situation grew increasingly precarious. In April 1918, they were moved to the Ipatiev House in Yekaterinburg, a grim prelude to their ultimate fate.

On the night of July 16-17, 1918, the Romanov family, along with their loyal retainers, were brutally executed by Bolshevik forces in the basement of the Ipatiev House. The official Soviet account claimed that Anastasia, along with her parents, siblings, and servants, were killed and their bodies disposed of in a clandestine manner. However, the chaotic nature of the execution and subsequent disposal of the bodies led to immediate speculation and rumors. The Bolsheviks, anxious to prevent any martyrdom or royalist rallying point, initially denied the killings, adding to the confusion.

In the aftermath of the execution, the location and fate of the Romanovs' remains were kept secret. For decades, the Soviet government maintained that the entire family had been killed, but conflicting reports and lack of concrete evidence fueled rumors of survivors. The most persistent and captivating of these rumors centered on Anastasia, suggesting that she had somehow escaped the massacre.

The first and most famous claimant to Anastasia's identity emerged in 1920. A young woman was rescued from a canal in Berlin, Germany, and taken to a mental hospital. She initially refused to reveal her identity, but over time she claimed to be Anastasia Romanov. Known as Anna Anderson, she bore a striking resemblance to the young princess and possessed intimate knowledge of the Romanov family and their court. Anderson's claims attracted significant attention and led to a protracted legal battle over her identity. While some Romanov relatives and acquaintances were convinced by her story, others remained skeptical, pointing out inconsistencies and questioning her motives.

Anna Anderson's case became a media sensation, inspiring books, films, and intense public interest. She lived a tumultuous life, moving between Europe and the United States, and was supported by various sympathizers who believed her claim. However, Anderson's identity remained controversial and unresolved until after her death in 1984. Advances in DNA testing in the 1990s finally allowed for a definitive answer. Analysis of a tissue sample from Anderson, compared with DNA from living Romanov relatives, conclusively proved that she was not related to the Romanovs. Instead, she was identified as Franziska Schanzkowska, a Polish factory worker with a history of mental illness.

While the case of Anna Anderson was the most famous, she was not the only claimant to Anastasia's identity. Over the years, several other women came forward, each with their own stories of miraculous escape and survival. None of these claims could be substantiated, and most were quickly dismissed as fabrications or delusions.

The mystery of Anastasia's fate took a significant turn in the late 20th century. In 1979, amateur historians discovered a shallow grave near Yekaterinburg containing the remains of several individuals. However, it was not until after the collapse of the Soviet Union that the Russian government officially exhumed the site in 1991. DNA testing and forensic analysis confirmed that the remains belonged to the Romanov family, but two bodies were notably missing: those of Anastasia and her brother, Alexei.

The absence of Anastasia's and Alexei's remains fueled further speculation and hope that they might have survived. However, in 2007, another grave was discovered near the original burial site, containing the remains of two young individuals. Subsequent DNA testing confirmed that these remains were those of Anastasia and Alexei, conclusively proving that all members of the immediate Romanov family had perished in 1918.

Despite the definitive identification of the Romanov remains, the legend of Anastasia's possible survival continues to capture the popular imagination. The story of a lost princess escaping a brutal fate resonates deeply, tapping into themes of resilience, hope, and the enduring human spirit. The animated film "Anastasia" (1997) and various other cultural depictions have kept the myth alive, often blurring the lines between historical fact and romantic fiction.

The broader context of the Romanov family's tragic end is deeply intertwined with the seismic shifts in Russian society and politics during the early 20th century. The fall of the Romanovs marked the end of the imperial era and the beginning of Soviet rule, a period characterized by radical ideological changes and profound social upheaval. The brutal execution of the Romanov family symbolized the violent overthrow of the old order and the establishment of a new, revolutionary regime.

In addition to the political implications, the story of Anastasia and her family highlights the personal dimensions of historical events. The Romanovs were not merely figures of political power but a family with complex relationships, hopes, and fears. Their personal letters, diaries, and photographs reveal a deeply human side to the grand narrative of history, making their tragic end all the more poignant.

Chapter 43: The Mystery of the Black Donnellys

The mystery of the Black Donnellys is a tale steeped in violence, legend, and enduring intrigue. It revolves around the Donnelly family, Irish immigrants who settled in the township of Biddulph, near London, Ontario, in the mid-19th century. The family's brutal massacre on February 4, 1880, and the subsequent trials and continuing mystery of their fate have left a lasting imprint on Canadian folklore and history. The story encompasses themes of immigration, prejudice, frontier justice, and community tensions, making it a complex and multifaceted narrative that continues to captivate and mystify.

The Donnelly family patriarch, James Donnelly, emigrated from Tipperary, Ireland, in 1842, bringing with him his wife Johannah and their children. Like many Irish immigrants of the time, the Donnellys were fleeing the Great Famine and the political and economic turmoil in Ireland. They settled on a plot of land in Biddulph Township, a rough and rugged area known for its harsh living conditions and lawlessness. James Donnelly, determined and strong-willed, was not one to shy away from conflict, and this trait would define much of the family's interactions with their neighbors.

Conflict and controversy seemed to follow the Donnellys from the outset. James Donnelly was involved in a dispute over land ownership shortly after their arrival, which set the stage for ongoing feuds with neighbors. In 1857, he was convicted of murdering Patrick Farrell during a violent altercation. The incident stemmed from a dispute over a timber contract and further inflamed local tensions. Donnelly was sentenced to be hanged but had his sentence commuted to seven years in Kingston Penitentiary, returning to Biddulph Township upon his release. This violent episode marked the beginning of a series of clashes between the Donnelly family and the local community.

The Donnellys' reputation in Biddulph was fraught with allegations of criminal behavior, ranging from arson and theft to assault and murder. Some of these accusations were likely true, while others were fueled by prejudice and the family's notorious reputation. The Donnellys were seen by many as a disruptive and dangerous presence, leading to a cycle of retaliation and retribution between them and their neighbors. The family was known to be fiercely protective of their land and interests, often resorting to violence to defend themselves against perceived threats.

Central to the tensions in Biddulph was the phenomenon of the vigilante justice that took root in the community. The so-called "Biddulph Peace Society" or the "Whiteboys," named after a secret Irish agrarian organization, emerged as a group dedicated to curbing the Donnellys' influence. This vigilante group, composed of local settlers, took it upon themselves to administer justice as they saw fit, often through extralegal means. The presence of this group highlighted the deep divisions and the breakdown of lawful order in the township, where official law enforcement was sparse and often ineffective.

The simmering animosity reached its tragic climax in the early hours of February 4, 1880. A mob, reportedly numbering around 20 to 30 men, descended upon the Donnelly homestead armed with clubs and other weapons. They set fire to the house and brutally murdered five members of the Donnelly family: James, Johannah, their sons Thomas and John, and their niece Bridget. The scene was one of horrific violence, with the victims being beaten and burned beyond recognition. The massacre was a culmination of years of pent-up hatred and hostility, and it shocked the local community and the wider region.

The immediate aftermath of the massacre saw a flurry of legal activity, with several men arrested and charged with the murders. However, the trials were mired in controversy and plagued by witness intimidation, conflicting testimonies, and a pervasive sense of fear among the local population. The first trial, held in London, Ontario, ended in a hung jury, and a second trial resulted in an acquittal. The failure to convict anyone for the murders left a lingering sense of injustice and unresolved tension in the community. Many believed that the trials were tainted by the influence of the vigilante group and the widespread fear of retribution.

The enduring mystery of the Black Donnellys extends beyond the immediate violence of their deaths to the broader social and cultural implications of their story. The narrative has become a part of Canadian folklore, with numerous books, plays, and even a television miniseries exploring the events and their legacy. The Donnelly story raises questions about the nature of justice, the impact of community prejudice, and the ways in which history is remembered and mythologized. The Donnellys have been portrayed variously as victims of brutal frontier justice, as dangerous criminals who reaped what they sowed, and as tragic figures caught in the tumult of a violent and lawless time.

One of the most significant aspects of the Donnelly legacy is the way it reflects broader themes of immigration and cultural conflict. The Donnellys, as Irish immigrants, were part of a larger wave of newcomers to Canada who often faced significant challenges in integrating into their new communities. The prejudice and hostility they encountered in Biddulph were not unique but part of a larger pattern of xenophobia and resistance to change that characterized many frontier settlements. The story of the Donnellys thus serves as a lens through which to examine the broader experiences of immigrants in North America and the ways in which cultural tensions can escalate into violence.

The physical remnants of the Donnelly story also continue to draw interest. The site of the Donnelly homestead, now a museum, attracts visitors and history enthusiasts who seek to connect with the tangible aspects of the past. The grave markers of the Donnelly family in St.

Patrick's Cemetery are a poignant reminder of the human cost of the violence and the enduring impact of the events on the local community. These sites serve as focal points for reflection and remembrance, highlighting the ways in which history is preserved and interpreted.

In recent years, historians and researchers have continued to explore the Donnelly story, uncovering new details and perspectives that add depth and nuance to the narrative. Contemporary scholarship has sought to move beyond the simplistic dichotomies of victim and villain, instead examining the complex social dynamics and individual motivations that shaped the events. This more nuanced approach helps to humanize the participants and provides a richer understanding of the historical context in which the Donnelly saga unfolded.

The mystery of the Black Donnellys, with its blend of fact and folklore, remains a powerful and compelling story that continues to resonate with audiences. It is a tale that speaks to the darker aspects of human nature, the complexities of community life, and the enduring power of narrative to shape our understanding of the past. The Donnelly story challenges us to grapple with difficult questions about justice, memory, and the ways in which we confront and make sense of historical violence.

Chapter 44: The Mysterious Passing of Brittany Murphy

The mysterious passing of Brittany Murphy, a talented and beloved actress, singer, and performer, remains one of Hollywood's most perplexing and heartbreaking stories. Born on November 10, 1977, in Atlanta, Georgia, Brittany Anne Bertolotti, later known as Brittany Murphy, grew up with dreams of stardom. Her vibrant personality, distinctive voice, and undeniable talent quickly set her apart, leading her to a successful career in film and television. However, her sudden and untimely death on December 20, 2009, at the age of 32, sparked a whirlwind of speculation, conspiracy theories, and unanswered questions that continue to linger over a decade later.

Brittany Murphy's career began in the early 1990s with roles in television series such as "Blossom" and "Sister, Sister." However, it was her breakout role in the 1995 cult classic "Clueless" that catapulted her to fame. Murphy's portrayal of Tai Frasier, the endearing and awkward new girl, showcased her comedic timing and charm, earning her widespread recognition. She continued to build on this success with notable performances in films like "Girl, Interrupted" (1999), "8 Mile" (2002), and "Sin City" (2005). Murphy's versatility as an actress allowed her to tackle a wide range of genres, from romantic comedies to intense dramas, solidifying her reputation as a talented and dynamic performer.

Despite her professional success, Brittany Murphy's personal life was often marred by challenges and controversies. Her relationships, particularly her marriage to screenwriter Simon Monjack in 2007, were frequently scrutinized by the media. Monjack, who had a history of legal and financial troubles, was seen by many as a negative influence on Murphy. Reports of their tumultuous relationship, coupled with rumors of substance abuse and erratic behavior, painted a picture of a star struggling behind the scenes. Friends and colleagues expressed concern over Murphy's well-being, noting significant changes in her appearance and demeanor in the years leading up to her death.

The events surrounding Brittany Murphy's death were both sudden and bewildering. On the morning of December 20, 2009, she was found unresponsive in the bathroom of her Hollywood Hills home by her mother, Sharon Murphy. Despite efforts to revive her, Murphy was pronounced dead at Cedars-Sinai Medical Center in Los Angeles. The initial shock of her passing was compounded by the vague and inconclusive nature of the early reports. The Los Angeles County Coroner's office eventually ruled her death as accidental, citing the primary cause as pneumonia, with contributing factors of iron-deficiency anemia and multiple drug intoxication.

The coroner's report indicated that Murphy had been suffering from a severe respiratory infection, which, combined with her weakened state due to anemia, proved fatal. The multiple drugs found in her system were all legal and included over-the-counter medications, prescription drugs, and supplements. The combination of these substances, intended to treat her symptoms, ultimately overwhelmed her already compromised health. However, this explanation did little to quell the rampant speculation and conspiracy theories that emerged in the wake of her death.

One of the most pervasive theories suggested that Brittany Murphy had been poisoned. This theory gained traction when her husband, Simon Monjack, died under similar circumstances just five months later, in May 2010. Monjack's death was also attributed to pneumonia and anemia, leading some to speculate about a more sinister cause. The similarities in their deaths, coupled with reports of toxic mold in their home, fueled suspicions of foul play. Murphy's father, Angelo Bertolotti, was a vocal proponent of this theory, alleging that his daughter had been murdered and pushing for further investigation.

In 2013, Bertolotti obtained independent toxicology testing of hair samples from Murphy, which reportedly found high levels of heavy metals consistent with rat poison. These findings reignited public interest and media scrutiny, but were met with skepticism by medical experts and law enforcement officials. The Los Angeles County Coroner's office stood by its original findings, dismissing the new test results as inconclusive and suggesting that environmental factors or hair treatments could account for the elevated metal levels. Despite Bertolotti's persistent efforts, no new evidence emerged to substantiate the poisoning theory.

The role of Simon Monjack in Brittany Murphy's life and death also remained a topic of intense debate. Monjack, a British screenwriter and producer, was a controversial figure with a troubled past. Prior to his relationship with Murphy, he had been involved in multiple legal disputes and faced allegations of fraud and financial misconduct. His sudden marriage to Murphy and his subsequent control over her career and finances raised eyebrows among her friends and colleagues. In the aftermath of her death, Monjack's behavior and statements further fueled suspicions. He reportedly exhibited erratic behavior, made contradictory claims about Murphy's health, and appeared to exploit her memory for financial gain.

Monjack's death, coming so soon after Murphy's, added another layer of complexity to the case. Some speculated that Monjack's involvement in criminal activities or connections to dangerous individuals might have played a role in their untimely deaths. Others pointed to the possibility of a shared underlying health condition, perhaps exacerbated by environmental factors such as the alleged toxic mold in their home. The sudden loss of both Murphy and Monjack left many questions unanswered, and the true nature of their relationship and its impact on her life and career remains a subject of conjecture.

The media's role in Brittany Murphy's life and death cannot be overlooked. Throughout her career, she was often the subject of tabloid speculation and gossip, with her personal struggles and relationships frequently splashed across headlines. In death, the sensationalism continued, with various outlets perpetuating unfounded rumors and conspiracy theories. This constant media scrutiny not only contributed to the public's fascination with her story but also complicated efforts to uncover the truth. The intersection of fame, privacy, and public curiosity created a toxic environment that both fueled and obscured the mystery surrounding her death.

In the years since Brittany Murphy's passing, her legacy has been reassessed by both fans and critics. While her tragic end often overshadows her achievements, it is important to remember the talent and charisma that defined her career. Murphy's performances, marked by a unique blend of vulnerability and strength, left an indelible mark on the entertainment industry. Films like "Clueless," "8 Mile," and "Girl, Interrupted" continue to resonate with audiences, showcasing her versatility and depth as an actress. Her voice work in animated projects such as "King of the Hill" and "Happy Feet" also highlighted her range and ability to bring characters to life.

The mystery of Brittany Murphy's death also serves as a cautionary tale about the pressures of fame and the vulnerabilities of those in the public eye. Her story underscores the importance of mental health, the dangers of self-medication, and the need for support systems in the often unforgiving world of Hollywood. The unresolved questions and lingering doubts about her death remind us of the complexities and challenges faced by those who navigate the intersection of personal and professional lives under constant scrutiny.

Chapter 45: The Death of Amy Winehouse

The death of Amy Winehouse, one of the most influential and enigmatic figures in contemporary music, remains a poignant and tragic story. Born on September 14, 1983, in Southgate, London, Amy Jade Winehouse grew up in a family deeply immersed in music. Her father, Mitchell Winehouse, was a taxi driver and amateur singer, while her mother, Janis Winehouse, was a pharmacist. Amy's natural talent for singing and songwriting became evident at an early age, leading her to pursue a career in music that would bring her international fame and acclaim. However, her life and career were also marked by personal struggles, addiction, and ultimately, her untimely death on July 23, 2011, at the age of 27.

Winehouse's early years were characterized by a love for music, influenced by a diverse range of genres, from jazz and soul to rhythm and blues. She attended the Sylvia Young Theatre School, where her exceptional vocal abilities stood out. At the age of 16, she was discovered by a talent scout, leading to a recording contract with Island Records. In 2003, Winehouse released her debut album, "Frank," which showcased her distinctive voice and songwriting prowess. The album received critical acclaim and established her as a rising star in the music industry.

However, it was her second album, "Back to Black," released in 2006, that catapulted Winehouse to global stardom. The album, produced by Mark Ronson, featured a fusion of classic soul, jazz, and contemporary pop, and included hits like "Rehab," "You Know I'm No Good," and the title track "Back to Black." Winehouse's raw and emotionally charged lyrics, combined with her powerful and soulful voice, resonated with audiences worldwide. The album's success earned her numerous awards, including five Grammy Awards in 2008, making her the first British woman to win five Grammys in a single night.

Despite her professional success, Amy Winehouse's personal life was plagued by turmoil and instability. Her struggles with addiction to alcohol and drugs were well-documented and became a focal point of media attention. Winehouse's tumultuous relationship with Blake Fielder-Civil, whom she married in 2007, was marked by public displays of affection and conflict, further fueling tabloid speculation. Fielder-Civil later admitted to introducing Winehouse to hard drugs, which exacerbated her addiction issues.

Winehouse's battle with substance abuse and mental health issues had a profound impact on her career and public image. Her erratic behavior, missed performances, and legal troubles became regular fodder for the press, overshadowing her musical achievements. The intense media scrutiny and public fascination with her personal struggles contributed to a cycle of self-destructive behavior, as Winehouse attempted to cope with the pressures of fame and her inner demons.

In the years leading up to her death, Amy Winehouse made several attempts to overcome her addiction and regain control of her life. She entered rehab multiple times and took breaks from her career to focus on her health. However, these efforts were often short-lived, and Winehouse continued to struggle with the demands of sobriety and the emotional turmoil that accompanied her addiction. Despite her ongoing battles, she remained a beloved figure in the music industry, with fans and peers alike recognizing her immense talent and potential.

On July 23, 2011, Amy Winehouse was found dead in her London home by her bodyguard. The initial shock of her death sent ripples through the music world and beyond, as fans and fellow artists mourned the loss of a unique and influential voice. The subsequent investigation revealed that Winehouse had died of alcohol poisoning, with a blood alcohol level more than five times the legal driving limit.

The coroner's report classified her death as "death by misadventure," indicating that it was an accidental and tragic consequence of her excessive drinking.

Winehouse's death at the age of 27 placed her in the infamous "27 Club," a group of iconic musicians who died at the same age, including Jimi Hendrix, Janis Joplin, Jim Morrison, and Kurt Cobain. This eerie coincidence further cemented her status as a tragic and legendary figure in music history. The circumstances of her death highlighted the devastating impact of addiction and the challenges faced by those in the public eye who struggle with substance abuse.

In the aftermath of her death, Amy Winehouse's legacy has been shaped by both her musical contributions and the tragic narrative of her life. Her posthumous releases, including the compilation album "Lioness: Hidden Treasures" (2011) and the documentary "Amy" (2015), have helped to preserve and celebrate her artistic achievements. The documentary, directed by Asif Kapadia, provided an intimate and unflinching look at Winehouse's life, chronicling her rise to fame, her personal struggles, and her untimely death. The film received critical acclaim and won the Academy Award for Best Documentary Feature, bringing renewed attention to Winehouse's story and her impact on music and culture.

Winehouse's influence on contemporary music and artists is undeniable. Her distinctive voice, deeply personal lyrics, and fusion of genres have inspired a new generation of musicians. Artists such as Adele, Lady Gaga, and Sam Smith have cited Winehouse as a significant influence on their work, praising her authenticity and emotional depth. Her ability to convey raw emotion and vulnerability through her music has left an indelible mark on the industry, challenging artists to embrace their individuality and express their truth.

Beyond her musical legacy, Amy Winehouse's story has also raised important conversations about mental health, addiction, and the pressures of fame. Her struggles have underscored the need for greater awareness and support for artists dealing with similar issues. The Amy Winehouse Foundation, established by her family in 2011, aims to provide support and education for young people struggling with addiction and mental health challenges. The foundation's work serves as a testament to Winehouse's enduring impact and the efforts to turn her tragic story into a force for positive change.

In reflecting on Amy Winehouse's life and career, it is essential to recognize the complexities and contradictions that defined her. She was a gifted artist whose music touched millions, yet she also grappled with profound personal challenges. Her story is one of immense talent and creativity, but also one of vulnerability and pain. Winehouse's ability to channel her experiences into her music created a deep connection with her audience, allowing her to transcend her struggles and leave a lasting legacy.

The death of Amy Winehouse remains a deeply tragic chapter in the history of contemporary music. Her passing at the age of 27 cut short a career that had already made a significant impact and held the promise of even greater achievements. As fans and the music community continue to celebrate her contributions, they also grapple with the lessons of her life and the importance of supporting those who face similar struggles. Amy Winehouse's story is a poignant reminder of the fragility of life, the power of music, and the enduring quest for understanding and compassion.

Chapter 46: The Enigma of the Greenbrier Ghost

The Enigma of the Greenbrier Ghost stands as one of the most fascinating and mysterious tales in the annals of American folklore and legal history. This peculiar story from the late 19th century intertwines supernatural elements with judicial proceedings, making it a unique case where a ghost's testimony allegedly led to a murder conviction.

In the rural, mountainous region of Greenbrier County, West Virginia, the narrative of the Greenbrier Ghost begins with the life and untimely death of Zona Heaster Shue. Born Elva Zona Heaster in the mid-1870s, she was a young woman who lived a relatively ordinary life until she met and married Erasmus "Edward" Shue in October 1896. Edward, a blacksmith by trade, had recently moved to the area, bringing with him a somewhat mysterious past. Despite whispers of previous marriages and a checkered history, he and Zona seemed to lead a happy life.

However, this semblance of normalcy was shattered on January 23, 1897, when Zona's lifeless body was discovered at her home. The discovery was made by a young boy who had been sent on an errand by Edward. Zona was found lying at the foot of the stairs, seemingly having succumbed to a tragic accident. Her body was positioned awkwardly, with her head resting on one side, an arm across her chest, and her legs stretched out straight. The scene suggested she had fallen down the stairs.

The local doctor, George W. Knapp, was summoned and conducted a cursory examination. Although initially concluding that Zona had died from "an everlasting faint" or heart failure, Dr. Knapp later revised his statement to "complications from childbirth" after being pressured by Edward. This conclusion was dubious, as there were no indications Zona was pregnant, and the doctor's examination was notably superficial. Edward's insistence on Zona's burial proceeding quickly and his peculiar behavior during her wake further aroused suspicion. He dressed her in a high-collared dress and a veil, preventing a thorough examination of her body, and he exhibited odd behavior by cradling Zona's head, showing an unusual level of distress and protectiveness over her neck and head area.

Zona's mother, Mary Jane Heaster, never believed the official story of her daughter's death. She was convinced that foul play was involved, specifically suspecting Edward. Overcome with grief and determined to uncover the truth, she prayed fervently for her daughter to reveal the true circumstances of her death. According to legend, Mary Jane's prayers were answered when Zona's spirit appeared to her over four consecutive nights. The ghostly apparition provided chilling details of her murder, claiming that Edward had killed her in a fit of rage by breaking her neck after she failed to prepare a satisfactory dinner. The ghost reportedly twisted its head around to demonstrate the extent of the injury, solidifying Mary Jane's resolve to seek justice for her daughter.

Armed with this spectral testimony, Mary Jane persuaded the local prosecutor, John Alfred Preston, to reopen the case. Skeptical at first, Preston eventually exhumed Zona's body for a thorough autopsy. The examination, conducted by Dr. Knapp and two other physicians, revealed that Zona's neck had indeed been broken, and her windpipe was crushed, findings consistent with the ghost's claims. These injuries could not have been caused by a fall down the stairs and strongly indicated foul play.

Edward Shue was promptly arrested and charged with Zona's murder. During the trial, Mary Jane Heaster testified about her supernatural experiences, stating that Zona's ghost had visited her and revealed the circumstances of her death. Remarkably, the judge allowed this testimony, albeit with the instruction to the jury to consider it only as they saw fit, given its supernatural nature. Despite the extraordinary nature of Mary Jane's testimony, the physical evidence of Zona's injuries, combined with Edward's suspicious behavior and dubious past, was compelling. Edward's prior marriages ended under mysterious circumstances, and he had a history of violence, further incriminating him. The jury found Edward Shue guilty of murder, and he was sentenced to life imprisonment. He died a few years later in the West Virginia State Penitentiary, his death attributed to an unknown epidemic that swept through the prison.

The Greenbrier Ghost case remains a singular occurrence in American legal history, notable for being possibly the only case where the testimony of a ghost was a pivotal factor in securing a murder conviction. The story has captivated imaginations and has been passed down through generations, cementing its place in local folklore. While some view it as a genuine account of supernatural intervention, others see it as a tale of a mother's determination and intuition leading to the uncovering of a murder.

The case raises intriguing questions about the interplay between folklore, justice, and the supernatural. It highlights the ways in which cultural beliefs and legal proceedings can intersect in unexpected ways. The story of the Greenbrier Ghost continues to be a topic of interest for historians, paranormal enthusiasts, and legal scholars, who are fascinated by its unique blend of mystery, tragedy, and the supernatural. Whether viewed as a testament to the power of maternal intuition or as a fascinating legal anomaly, the Greenbrier Ghost endures as an enigmatic and compelling tale from the past.

Chapter 47: The Disappearance of Emanuela Orlandi

The enigmatic disappearance of Emanuela Orlandi is one of Italy's most perplexing and enduring mysteries, intertwining elements of conspiracy, organized crime, Vatican intrigue, and high-level political machinations. On June 22, 1983, 15-year-old Emanuela Orlandi, a Vatican citizen and daughter of a prominent Vatican employee, vanished without a trace after leaving her family's apartment within Vatican City to attend a music lesson in Rome. What began as a seemingly straightforward missing person case soon spiraled into a labyrinthine saga marked by bizarre leads, cryptic messages, and unsubstantiated rumors, capturing global attention and leaving investigators grappling for answers for decades.

Emanuela's disappearance came at a time when tensions were high in Italy, with the country grappling with terrorism, organized crime, and political corruption. Emanuela, the fourth of five children, was described as a quiet and shy girl, deeply embedded in the fabric of the close-knit Vatican community. Her father, Ercole Orlandi, held a trusted position within the Prefecture of the Papal Household, overseeing the Pope's public audiences and ceremonies. This connection to the Vatican elevated the significance of her disappearance, making it a matter of not just personal tragedy but of considerable public and political interest.

The last known sighting of Emanuela occurred in the heart of Rome, after her music lesson at the Tommaso Ludovico Da Victoria School. She had called her sister, Federica, from a public phone booth, mentioning an offer from a man selling Avon cosmetics who proposed that she work for him. Despite her sister's advice to discuss it at home, Emanuela never returned. Witnesses later reported seeing her talking to a man in a green BMW, but after that, her trail went cold.

The initial investigation was marred by delays and confusion, with the Orlandi family receiving numerous phone calls, many of which were from pranksters or individuals providing false leads. Among these, one call stood out, from a man identifying himself as "Pierluigi," who claimed that Emanuela had been abducted by an extremist group demanding the release of Mehmet Ali Ağca, the Turkish gunman who attempted to assassinate Pope John Paul II in 1981. This lead introduced the first of many conspiracy theories linking Emanuela's disappearance to broader geopolitical events.

A few days later, another mysterious caller, "Mario," also tied Emanuela's fate to the release of Ağca, adding weight to the theory that she had been kidnapped as a bargaining chip to secure his freedom. The claim was bolstered by a letter received by the Orlandi family, purportedly from an organization called the "Turkish Anti-Christian Liberation Front," which repeated the demand for Ağca's release. However, despite these apparent leads, no concrete evidence ever surfaced to substantiate the connection, and the motives behind Emanuela's disappearance remained obscure.

The investigation took a bizarre turn in 1984 when an anonymous caller to a prominent Italian television program claimed that Emanuela was being held in a convent in Luxembourg. This prompted a flurry of media attention and further complicated the already convoluted case. Subsequent searches and inquiries proved fruitless, and the caller's identity and motives remained unknown, adding to the growing air of mystery and speculation.

Over the years, numerous theories emerged, ranging from plausible to fantastical, each adding new layers of intrigue and complexity. One theory posited that Emanuela had been abducted by a faction within the Vatican itself, possibly as part of a power struggle or to blackmail the Church over financial or political matters. This theory was given credence by some investigators and journalists who pointed to the Vatican's opaque financial dealings and internal rivalries, suggesting that Emanuela's disappearance might be linked to efforts to exert pressure on high-ranking Vatican officials.

Another theory connected her disappearance to the Roman underworld, particularly to the Banda della Magliana, a notorious criminal gang with alleged ties to the Vatican Bank and prominent Italian politicians. According to this theory, Emanuela was kidnapped as leverage in negotiations over substantial sums of money owed by the Vatican to the gang, highlighting the murky intersection of organized crime and institutional corruption in Italy during the 1980s.

Further complicating the case was the involvement of high-profile individuals who either made claims about or were implicated in the mystery. In 2005, a former Turkish counterintelligence operative, Abuzer Ugurlu, alleged that Emanuela was alive and living in Turkey. This claim, though unsubstantiated, rekindled interest in the Turkish connection and the possibility of international conspiracies involving the KGB, the CIA, and various intelligence agencies.

The case took another dramatic turn in 2012 when an Italian journalist, Gianluigi Nuzzi, published letters from a Vatican insider that hinted at a cover-up involving Emanuela's fate. These documents suggested that she might have been hidden in a remote location, with high-level Vatican officials complicit in her abduction. The revelations prompted renewed calls for transparency and accountability from the Vatican, which had consistently denied any involvement in or knowledge of the case.

In 2018, the discovery of human remains during renovations at the Vatican's Nunciature in Rome sparked speculation that Emanuela's body had finally been found. However, forensic analysis later confirmed that the remains did not belong to her. The following year, Emanuela's family received an anonymous tip suggesting that her remains might be located in the Teutonic Cemetery within Vatican City. The ensuing excavation revealed several sets of bones, but none matched Emanuela's DNA, further deepening the mystery.

Emanuela's disappearance remains an open wound for her family and a haunting enigma for investigators and the public alike. Despite the numerous leads, theories, and media attention over the past four decades, the truth behind her vanishing remains elusive. The case has not only captivated Italy but also resonated globally, symbolizing the enduring human desire for truth and justice in the face of overwhelming uncertainty and the dark shadows cast by institutional secrecy and power.

The disappearance of Emanuela Orlandi continues to inspire speculation and debate, with new theories and revelations periodically emerging. The case underscores the complexity and opacity of the forces at play, whether they involve organized crime, international espionage, or the intricate politics of the Vatican. As each new lead emerges and inevitably leads to a dead end, the story of Emanuela Orlandi serves as a poignant reminder of the enduring mysteries that can lie beneath the surface of even the most seemingly ordinary lives, and the profound impact these mysteries can have on families, communities, and entire nations.

Chapter 48: The Unsolved Murder of Mary Phagan

The unsolved murder of Mary Phagan is one of the most notorious and controversial cases in American history, highlighting issues of racial tension, judicial corruption, and societal prejudices in the early 20th century South. Mary Phagan, a 13-year-old girl, was brutally murdered in Atlanta, Georgia, in 1913. The case not only captivated the nation but also exposed the deep divisions within American society and set the stage for profound social and legal changes.

Mary Phagan was born on June 1, 1899, in Florence, Alabama. She moved with her family to Marietta, Georgia, where her father, John Phagan, died when she was just a toddler. Her mother, Frances "Fannie" Phagan, remarried and the family relocated to Atlanta in search of better opportunities. Mary eventually found work at the National Pencil Company factory, where she assembled metal tips for pencils, a job that paid about 10 cents an hour. The factory was managed by Leo Frank, a Jewish man from New York who had moved to Atlanta to oversee operations.

On April 26, 1913, Mary Phagan went to the factory to collect her paycheck, as she was laid off due to a lack of supplies. It was Confederate Memorial Day, a significant holiday in the South, and the city was bustling with activities and parades. Mary never returned home that day. Her body was discovered early the next morning in the factory basement by the night watchman, Newt Lee. She had been strangled with a piece of her own lace, and her body showed signs of a brutal assault.

The investigation began under the supervision of the Atlanta Police Department and quickly attracted media attention. The public was outraged by the crime, and there was immense pressure to find the culprit. Initial suspicion fell on Newt Lee, the African American night watchman who discovered the body. However, discrepancies in his story and lack of concrete evidence led the authorities to release him, although racial prejudices at the time meant he remained under suspicion by many.

Attention soon turned to Leo Frank, the factory superintendent. Frank was an educated and relatively affluent Northern Jew, a stark contrast to the predominantly Christian, working-class Southern population of Atlanta. This cultural and religious difference made him an outsider and an easy target for public suspicion. Several factory workers, including 14-year-old Alonzo Mann, provided testimony that seemed to implicate Frank, though their accounts were contradictory and inconsistent.

As the investigation proceeded, another suspect emerged: Jim Conley, an African American janitor at the factory. Conley was found washing red stains from his shirt on the day Mary's body was discovered, and he initially claimed they were rust. Under interrogation, Conley changed his story multiple times. Ultimately, he confessed to helping Frank dispose of Mary's body, alleging that Frank had killed her in his office and then called him to assist with the cover-up. Conley's testimony was critical to the case against Frank, despite his dubious reliability and history of criminal behavior.

The trial of Leo Frank began in July 1913, presided over by Judge Leonard S. Roan. The courtroom was packed with spectators, reflecting the intense public interest and media frenzy surrounding the case. The prosecution, led by Hugh Dorsey, painted Frank as a sexual predator who lured Mary to his office under the pretext of discussing her job, assaulted her, and then murdered her when she resisted. Dorsey's arguments were bolstered by Jim Conley's testimony, which depicted Frank as the mastermind behind the crime. Conley's story, despite its inconsistencies, resonated with the jury and the public due to the racial and social dynamics of the time.

Frank's defense, led by Luther Rosser and Reuben Arnold, attempted to discredit Conley and argued that the evidence against Frank was circumstantial and insufficient. They highlighted Frank's clean record and his character references from prominent community members. However, their efforts were hampered by widespread anti-Semitic sentiments and the sensationalized portrayal of Frank in the media. The atmosphere in the courtroom was highly charged, with crowds outside chanting for Frank's conviction.

After a month-long trial, the jury, composed entirely of white men, deliberated for just a few hours before finding Leo Frank guilty of murder. He was sentenced to death by hanging. The verdict was met with jubilation by the public, who saw it as a victory for justice and retribution for Mary Phagan's death. However, the case was far from over.

Frank's legal team launched a series of appeals, arguing that the trial had been unfair and influenced by public pressure and media bias. They pointed to irregularities in the trial proceedings and the questionable reliability of Conley's testimony. The case went all the way to the United States Supreme Court, which narrowly upheld the conviction in a 7-2 decision. Despite this, Frank's attorneys continued to fight for his life, seeking a commutation of his death sentence.

In 1915, Georgia Governor John M. Slaton, after a thorough review of the case and the evidence, commuted Frank's sentence to life imprisonment, citing concerns about the fairness of the trial and the possibility of Frank's innocence. This decision was highly controversial and provoked a furious backlash. Many in Georgia viewed it as a miscarriage of justice and an affront to the memory of Mary Phagan.

In the wake of the commutation, anti-Semitic sentiments and public outrage reached a boiling point. On August 16, 1915, a group of about 25 men, who later came to be known as the "Knights of Mary Phagan," broke into the state prison farm where Frank was being held and abducted him. They transported him to Marietta, Mary's hometown, and lynched him the following morning. Frank's lynching was a brutal and shocking act of vigilante justice, and his body was later found hanging from a tree.

The aftermath of Frank's lynching had profound and lasting effects. It intensified racial and religious tensions in the South and led to the reformation of the Ku Klux Klan in Georgia. It also spurred the formation of the Anti-Defamation League (ADL), a Jewish organization dedicated to combating anti-Semitism and defending civil rights. The case highlighted the deep-seated prejudices and systemic injustices that plagued the American legal system and society at large.

Decades later, new evidence and testimony emerged, casting doubt on Frank's guilt and suggesting that Jim Conley may have been the true culprit. In 1982, Alonzo Mann, who had been a young office boy at the factory at the time of the murder, came forward with a confession. He stated that he had seen Conley carrying Mary's body to the basement and that Conley had threatened to kill him if he told anyone. Mann's revelation, coming 69 years after the murder, provided significant support for the theory that Conley had acted alone and that Frank had been wrongly convicted.

In 1986, the Georgia State Board of Pardons and Paroles posthumously pardoned Leo Frank, not on the grounds of innocence but in recognition of the state's failure to protect him and ensure a fair trial. The case of Mary Phagan remains officially unsolved, with no definitive conclusion as to who was responsible for her murder.

The murder of Mary Phagan and the subsequent trial and lynching of Leo Frank continue to be subjects of intense scrutiny and debate. The case serves as a stark reminder of the dangers of mob mentality, the flaws in the judicial system, and the devastating impact of prejudice and discrimination. It also underscores the importance of due process and the need for vigilance in protecting the rights of all individuals, regardless of race, religion, or social status.

The legacy of the case lives on in various forms, from scholarly research and legal reforms to cultural depictions in literature, film, and theater. It remains a powerful symbol of the struggle for justice and the enduring quest to uncover the truth, even in the face of overwhelming societal and institutional challenges. The tragic story of Mary Phagan and Leo Frank continues to resonate, reminding us of the complex and often painful history that shapes our present and future.

Chapter 49: The Mysterious Death of Michael Rockefeller

The mysterious death of Michael Rockefeller remains one of the most enigmatic and controversial cases of the 20th century, blending elements of adventure, tragedy, and intrigue. The scion of one of America's wealthiest and most influential families, Michael Rockefeller disappeared in 1961 in the remote jungles of New Guinea, sparking a multitude of theories and speculation about his fate. His story is a tapestry of cultural exploration, dangerous curiosity, and the shadowy intersections of different worlds.

Michael Clark Rockefeller was born on May 18, 1938, into the prominent Rockefeller family, known for their vast wealth and significant contributions to American society. His father, Nelson Rockefeller, served as Governor of New York and later as Vice President of the United States. Despite his privileged background, Michael was drawn to a life of exploration and adventure, showing a keen interest in anthropology and art. After graduating from Harvard University in 1960, where he studied history and economics, Michael became increasingly fascinated with indigenous cultures, particularly those in the remote regions of New Guinea.

In the early 1960s, New Guinea, then part of the Dutch East Indies, was one of the world's last frontiers, home to diverse and largely uncontacted indigenous tribes. It was a land rich in unique cultural practices and art forms, which intrigued Michael. In 1961, he joined a Harvard-Peabody Museum expedition to study and collect artifacts from the island's indigenous peoples. This journey would prove to be both his greatest adventure and his final one.

On November 17, 1961, Michael and a Dutch anthropologist, René Wassing, embarked on an expedition to collect artifacts from the Asmat people, a tribe known for their intricate wood carvings and complex social structures. The Asmat lived in a swampy and remote area on the southern coast of New Guinea, largely isolated from the outside world. The two men set out in a 40-foot dugout canoe, accompanied by two local guides. As they navigated the turbulent Arafura Sea, their canoe was swamped and overturned, leaving them adrift approximately 12 miles from shore.

For some time, they clung to the canoe, hoping for rescue. However, as the hours passed and their situation became more desperate, Michael made a bold decision. Believing he could reach the shore, he told Wassing, "I think I can make it," and began swimming towards land, using two gasoline cans as flotation devices. This was the last time Michael Rockefeller was seen alive. Despite extensive search efforts by the Dutch authorities, American officials, and his own family, no trace of him was ever found.

The initial conclusion was that Michael had drowned or been eaten by sharks or crocodiles, common hazards in the region. However, the lack of a body and the mysterious circumstances surrounding his disappearance led to widespread speculation and the emergence of various theories about his fate. Some believed he had been captured or killed by local tribes, while others suggested he might have chosen to live among the indigenous people, adopting their way of life and disappearing into the jungle.

The Asmat people, whom Michael had been studying, were known for their complex rituals and practices, including headhunting and cannibalism, which were integral to their culture and social order. These practices, although shocking to outsiders, were deeply rooted in the Asmat's belief system and served important functions within their society. The possibility that Michael had encountered violence or ritualistic practices added a macabre dimension to the mystery of his disappearance.

In the years following Michael's disappearance, various accounts and rumors emerged, suggesting that he had been killed and possibly eaten by the Asmat. One of the most compelling pieces of evidence came from a Catholic priest, Cornelius Van Kessel, who reported hearing from locals that Michael had been killed by the Asmat in retaliation for a previous incident involving Dutch colonial authorities. According to this account, the Asmat viewed Michael as an outsider and an enemy, making him a target for ritualistic violence. This theory was later supported by accounts from missionaries and anthropologists who had worked in the region, although definitive proof was never found.

The Rockefeller family, driven by grief and a desire for answers, conducted their own investigations. Michael's twin sister, Mary Rockefeller Morgan, and his father, Nelson Rockefeller, made multiple trips to New Guinea, meeting with officials and local people in an effort to uncover the truth. Despite their efforts and the substantial resources at their disposal, the mystery remained unresolved, and the family eventually accepted that Michael was likely dead.

Over the decades, the case of Michael Rockefeller has continued to fascinate and perplex investigators, scholars, and the public. In 2014, journalist Carl Hoffman published a book titled "Savage Harvest," which presented new evidence suggesting that Michael had indeed been killed by the Asmat. Hoffman's investigation included interviews with surviving Asmat elders and examination of archival material, leading him to conclude that Michael had been ritually killed in retaliation for the actions of Dutch authorities, who had previously killed several Asmat men. Hoffman's book reignited interest in the case and added a new layer of complexity to the mystery, although it did not provide conclusive evidence to resolve the longstanding questions about Michael's fate.

The disappearance of Michael Rockefeller is a tale that intertwines cultural exploration with the perilous allure of the unknown. It highlights the dangers faced by those who venture into uncharted territories and the profound misunderstandings that can arise when different worlds collide. Michael's story is also a reflection of the complexities and challenges of cross-cultural encounters, particularly in the context of colonialism and its legacy.

The legacy of Michael Rockefeller's disappearance continues to resonate, raising important questions about the ethics of cultural exploration and the impact of Western contact on indigenous societies. It serves as a cautionary tale about the perils of hubris and the limits of human understanding, reminding us of the enduring mysteries that lie beyond the boundaries of our knowledge and experience. Michael's story is a poignant reminder of the fragility of life and the profound mysteries that can remain hidden in the most remote corners of the world.

Chapter 50: The Unsolved Case of the Isdal Woman

The unsolved case of the Isdal Woman, often referred to as one of Norway's greatest mysteries, involves the discovery of an unidentified woman's body in the Isdalen Valley near Bergen in 1970. This case has intrigued and perplexed investigators, journalists, and the public for over five decades, shrouded in an aura of secrecy, espionage, and unanswered questions. The Isdal Woman's enigmatic death is not only a gripping tale of intrigue but also a profound reflection of the complex geopolitical landscape of the Cold War era.

On November 29, 1970, a university professor and his two daughters were hiking in the Isdalen Valley, also known as "Death Valley" due to its reputation for suicides and accidents. During their hike, they stumbled upon the charred remains of a woman, lying among the rocks and bushes. The discovery was immediately reported to the Bergen police, who arrived at the scene to find a gruesome and puzzling sight. The woman's body was severely burned, with her arms in a boxer's pose, a typical reaction to severe heat. Nearby, they found several personal items, including a wristwatch, jewelry, and an umbrella, all of which were placed neatly around the body. Oddly, the labels on her clothes and belongings had been removed, and no identifying documents were found.

The initial examination of the scene suggested that the woman had died from a combination of burns and carbon monoxide poisoning. However, the circumstances surrounding her death raised numerous questions. Why was she in such a remote and dangerous area? Why were the labels removed from her clothes? And, most intriguingly, who was she, and what had led to her untimely demise?

The investigation quickly revealed more peculiarities. The autopsy showed that the woman had ingested around 50 to 70 sleeping pills, and her stomach contained traces of gasoline, indicating that she had either ingested or inhaled it before her death. Despite the extensive burns, there was no evidence of any other injuries or a struggle. The forensic analysis suggested that the woman was between 25 and 40 years old, of medium height and build, and likely of European descent. Her teeth had been extensively worked on, with distinctive dental work that was initially thought to be traceable. However, despite checking with international dental records, no match was found.

As the investigation deepened, the mystery only grew more complex. The police traced her movements to several hotels in Norway, where she had checked in under various aliases and nationalities. Hotel registers showed that she used at least eight different identities, including "Vera Jarle," "Claudia Tielt," and "Elizabeth Leenhouwer." She had also claimed to be from different countries, including Belgium, the Netherlands, and Germany. Each alias had a corresponding set of clothes and personal items, suggesting a deliberate attempt to obscure her identity.

Witnesses who had encountered the Isdal Woman described her as a striking and somewhat aloof individual, often seen wearing a wig and speaking multiple languages, including German, French, and English. Hotel staff noted that she frequently changed rooms and paid in cash, adding to the suspicion that she was trying to avoid leaving a traceable financial trail. Her behavior and the multiple identities she assumed suggested that she might have been involved in espionage or some other clandestine activity, a theory that was not far-fetched given the geopolitical tensions of the time.

The Cold War era was marked by intense espionage activities, with spies and covert agents operating across Europe. Norway, with its strategic location, was a hotspot for intelligence operations by both Western and Eastern bloc countries. The peculiar circumstances of the Isdal Woman's death, coupled with her multiple identities and secretive behavior, led many to speculate that she could have been a spy involved in a covert mission. This theory was further fueled by reports that she had been seen with unidentified men and that she had made cryptic notes in a notebook, which included a series of seemingly coded entries and telephone numbers.

As the investigation continued, the police discovered more clues that hinted at a connection to the espionage world. Among her belongings were a notepad with strange, code-like writing and a map with several locations marked, including military installations and sensitive areas. These findings led to speculation that the Isdal Woman might have been involved in intelligence gathering or surveillance activities, possibly for a foreign government. However, despite these leads, the investigation hit a dead end, with no concrete evidence to confirm her identity or the nature of her activities.

The case attracted significant media attention, both in Norway and internationally. Journalists and amateur sleuths alike delved into the mystery, uncovering additional details and theories about the Isdal Woman's background and possible connections. Some suggested that she might have been a member of a criminal organization or involved in illegal activities such as smuggling or drug trafficking. Others speculated that she could have been a victim of foul play, possibly related to personal or political motives.

One of the most intriguing aspects of the case was the Isdal Woman's meticulous efforts to conceal her identity. The removal of labels from her clothes, the use of multiple aliases, and the lack of identifying documents suggested a deliberate attempt to remain anonymous. This level of caution was consistent with the behavior of someone engaged in covert operations or trying to evade detection. However, despite extensive efforts by investigators to piece together her movements and contacts, the Isdal Woman's true identity and the reasons for her presence in Norway remained elusive.

In the years following the discovery, several theories have been proposed to explain the Isdal Woman's death. Some believe that she was a spy who was eliminated by intelligence operatives to prevent her from revealing sensitive information. Others suggest that she might have been involved in a covert mission that went wrong, leading to her death either through an accident or as a result of foul play. Another theory posits that she was a victim of a personal vendetta or a targeted assassination, possibly related to her activities or relationships.

In recent years, advances in forensic science and technology have renewed interest in the case. In 2017, Norwegian police exhumed the Isdal Woman's remains in an attempt to extract DNA and potentially identify her through modern genetic analysis. The results confirmed that she was of European descent, with genetic markers suggesting a possible origin in southern Europe. However, despite these advancements, no definitive match has been found, and the Isdal Woman's identity remains a mystery.

The case has also been the subject of several documentaries and investigative reports, which have brought new attention to the mystery and generated additional leads. In 2019, a team of Norwegian journalists published a podcast series titled "Death in Ice Valley," which explored the case in depth and uncovered new evidence and interviews. The series highlighted the enduring fascination with the Isdal Woman's story and the ongoing efforts to unravel the mystery of her death.

The unsolved case of the Isdal Woman continues to captivate the public imagination, serving as a reminder of the complexities and uncertainties of the human experience. Her enigmatic death is a reflection of the dark and hidden aspects of the Cold War era, where espionage, secrecy, and intrigue were commonplace. It also underscores the enduring mystery of the human condition and the lengths to which individuals will go to conceal their true identities and motives.

As the search for answers continues, the Isdal Woman's story remains a haunting and poignant reminder of the mysteries that lie beneath the surface of our world. Her death, shrouded in secrecy and intrigue, challenges us to question our assumptions and seek the truth, even in the face of uncertainty and ambiguity. The case of the Isdal Woman is a testament to the enduring power of mystery and the human desire to uncover the hidden truths that shape our lives and our history.

Epilogue

As we conclude this journey through the labyrinth of history's most perplexing deaths and disappearances, we are left with a profound sense of awe and contemplation. "The Mysteries of Historical Deaths: Investigating the Unsolved Enigmas" has taken us from the ancient world to modern times, revealing stories that continue to captivate and confound. Each case we have explored serves as a reminder of the fragility of life and the enduring allure of the unknown.

Throughout these chapters, we have encountered figures whose lives were as remarkable as their deaths were mysterious. From the vanished colony of Roanoke to the unresolved fate of Amelia Earhart, these enigmas have sparked countless theories and inspired generations of investigators, both amateur and professional. The persistence of these mysteries highlights our innate desire to seek truth and understanding, to piece together the puzzles left behind by time.

In examining these unsolved cases, we are reminded of the limitations of our knowledge and the boundless potential for discovery. Despite advances in science and technology, some questions remain tantalizingly out of reach, their answers obscured by the passage of time and the complexities of human nature. These enduring mysteries challenge us to remain curious and open-minded, to approach the unknown with a spirit of inquiry and humility.

The individuals whose stories we have recounted were more than the circumstances of their deaths; they were pioneers, leaders, artists, and dreamers. Their legacies continue to influence and inspire, even as their final moments remain shrouded in uncertainty. In remembering them, we honor not only their lives but also the enduring quest for truth that defines the human experience.

As we close this book, we carry with us the lessons learned from these enigmatic tales. We are reminded of the importance of critical thinking, the value of persistence, and the power of storytelling. These mysteries, though unsolved, serve as a testament to the resilience of the human spirit and the enduring pursuit of knowledge.

May the stories within these pages inspire future generations to continue the search for answers, to question the accepted narratives, and to explore the depths of the unknown. The mysteries of historical deaths are not merely puzzles to be solved; they are windows into the complexities of our past and mirrors reflecting our eternal quest for understanding.

Thank you for embarking on this journey with us. As we part ways, may you carry forward the spirit of curiosity and wonder, ever ready to delve into the mysteries that surround us. The enigmas of history may remain unresolved, but they remind us that the search for truth is a journey without end.

The End.